C000075491

JOINING THE DO

A Programme of Spiritual Reflection and

About the Author

Amalee Meehan, Ph.D. Boston College, taught science with Coláiste Iognáid, Galway, before joining Catholic Education, an Irish Schools Trust (**Ceist**), where she works in faith development. She teaches on the MA Christian Leadership in Education with Mary Immaculate College, University of Limerick, and is the co-author of two religious education textbooks for US Catholic High Schools as part of the *Credo* Series (Veritas, forthcoming).

JOINING THE DOTS

*A Programme of Spiritual Reflection
and Renewal for Educators*

Amalee Meehan
CEIST

VERITAS

Published 2012 by
Veritas Publications
7–8 Lower Abbey Street
Dublin 1, Ireland
publications@veritas.ie
www.veritas.ie

ISBN 978 1 84730 366 0
Copyright © CEIST, 2012

10 9 8 7 6 5 4 3 2 1

A catalogue record for this book is available from the British Library.

Designed by Barbara Croatto, Veritas
Printed in the Republic of Ireland by Gemini International, Dublin

Veritas books are printed on paper made from the wood pulp of
managed forests. For every tree felled, at least one tree is planted,
thereby renewing natural resources.

For teachers everywhere,
especially the staff of Ceist schools,
who give so much
to the lives of young people.

Contents

Preface

Standing in the Café Paradis in Cabo Roig, South East Spain, choosing *helado* with my two-year-old son, a woman approached me. Instead of the burst of Spanish I was expecting, she said, 'I think I know you. You came and spoke with us at the beginning of the school year last September. I'm from Presentation Secondary School in Limerick and we had a great *Joining the Dots* experience with you. We are still finding ourselves pulled between Martha and Mary – the polar temptations of a teacher's life.'

The woman was spot on. I had 'done' an adapted section of the programme with the staff of her school the previous autumn. *Joining the Dots* is an initiative in Christian theology and spirituality for educators. What my 'Spanish' friend was referring to occurs in Week 2 of the programme – a contemplation on the Scripture passage where Jesus visits the home of Martha and Mary.[1] It is a piece that teachers in particular really get to grips with as it reflects one of the inherent tensions in teaching – the pull towards action and the longing for contemplation. So often, the reality of daily life goes something like this: 'I am so busy running about all day – I go from class to class, group to group. I deal with maybe 240 students formally on any given day, and that's not counting the kids I meet in the corridors or the school yard. I am preparing, marking, and teaching, not to mention disciplining, listening, counselling, consoling, invigilating, examining, nursing, even parenting. It's all right for the "Marys" of this world, but I don't have time to sit at the feet of Jesus!'

Of course, as they tease it out, teachers come to realise that although the work of teaching might appear to be all Martha, there are many Mary moments too. There can always be contemplation in action, even in the most active of environments. Mary, in Luke's story, may have chosen the 'better part', but that is not always the case, nor is it the only part. As one member of the very first *Dots* group remarked, 'It is Martha, the woman on her feet, who opens the door; it is Martha who bids him welcome.'

Joining the Dots

Joining the Dots came about following a specific request to **ceist** (Catholic Education, an Irish Schools Trust)[2] for a programme that would offer teachers time out to reflect on their own spirituality and questions of faith. It began as a school-based programme with no fees, no travel and no exams. Over the space of two years, it has grown into a five-week programme for educators in Catholic settings – school and parish. By 'educators' in this context, I mean adult members of a school/parish community who are dealing with people in a teaching-learning environment – teachers, administrators and members of boards of management in schools, as well as parish educators and pastoral ministers. Of course, as primary educators of their children, the term also refers to parents.

In short, *Joining the Dots* is an invitation to people to explore their spirituality and connect it to their lives, including work lives, and to come to know for themselves the Christian ultimate value that is a personal lived relationship with God through Jesus Christ. Through connecting how God is revealed with the deep desires of the human heart, it hopes to deepen participants' own faith, praxis and relationships – with God, with themselves, and with others – especially in the context of a Christian community. In the Catholic Christian tradition, there is nothing in everyday life that is irrelevant to the spiritual life. The aim of the programme is to put this rich resource at the service of educators.

Joining the Dots does not presume the religious faith of the participant. Indeed, it is cognisant that, just as there is a diversity of students in Christian schools and settings, so there are educators of varying faith levels and from various faith traditions – and none. On the other hand, it is deeply rooted in the Christian tradition. It finds many ways to explore that tradition, for instance through music, art, literature, and particularly Scripture – both Hebrew and Christian.

Theological and spiritual content of *Joining the Dots*: A summary of the five weeks

1. *Joining the Dots* begins by breaking open the concept of spirituality and how an integrated spirituality can help us to live life with meaning. Week 1 identifies our longing for God which is a reflection of God's longing for us. It explores how God has been revealing Godself to humankind throughout history and is still doing so today. We can look in a special way to Sacred Scripture, to Church tradition, and to our own experience to help us know and take God's revelation to heart in our lives.

2. Week 2 explores the notion that if 'we teach who we are', then it is important that we know who we are and who we can be. It reflects on ourselves as educators, on the person of Jesus and on Jesus as educator. It concludes with the importance of being a reflective practitioner with Jesus Christ as model and mentor.

3. If Week 2 contends with 'who' we are, then Week 3 moves to explore 'whose' we are. It delves into the Creation myths and the concept of *Imago Dei* to reveal God as bountiful Creator and Loving Father. The third week explores the notion of *agape*, God as Love. It challenges participants to identify their own evolving images of God.

4. The Christocentric emphasis of the programme re-emerges in Week 4 centred around the mystery of the Incarnation. Participants explore the 2,000-year-old question *Cur Deus homo*. Jesus is the face of God and the Gospel message is incarnational. It reaches out to dialogue with human culture, just as Jesus did. We seek to inculturate the Gospel message in all its integrity in our time and culture, specifically in the education community.

5. The final week focuses on living and working from a Christian spirituality: what this means for the participants – individually and collectively, and for their school. Leaving room for the Spirit in the hustle and bustle of everyday life and engaging in spiritual practices are paramount in cultivating a healthy spirituality.

Thus the roots of the programme are Trinitarian, Christocentric and Incarnational. God the Spirit is the underlying emphasis of Weeks 1 and 5 so the conclusion of the programme feeds back to the beginning, emulating the cycle of life and the Spirit always and forever in our midst. God the Son is the focus of Weeks 2 and 4 – with the central mystery of the Incarnation highlighted specifically in Week 4; God the Father forms the emphasis of Week 3. Inculturation is central to the process – each week must resonate with the lived experience of participants and the reality of how Christian faith is expressed in their lives.

Prayer

Every week of *Joining the Dots* begins with silent prayer and reflective journaling. Every week concludes with a different prayer form to include:

- Contemplation on Scripture
- Guided meditation
- The examen
- Praying with music
- Communal prayer.

The hope is that every person will find one or more prayer forms that appeal to them which they can incorporate into a daily prayer habit.

Building on what already exists

One of the most important outcomes of *Joining the Dots* is deepening the bonds of community as it already exists. This is a great advantage of running the programme on site with members of the already extant school/parish community. The shared experience, shared language and shared understandings gained among participants are the hope for the future. Third-level programmes for Christian educators are often faced with the question: what happens when participants qualify and enter an education setting cut off from the learning community? When participants have finished a programme and are 'released back' to schools and parishes as isolated units, how can they keep up momentum; where do they go to refresh and reenergise? This is a question that has challenged third-level groups I have worked with such as the ACE Ireland programme with Notre Dame University, USA, or the MA in Christian Leadership in Education in Mary Immaculate College, Limerick. Online communities tend to have a very short life cycle, mostly because people miss the personal interaction, and because their actual work environments can differ greatly, the bonds of connection weaken. A school/parish based programme is able to address this difficulty.

How to approach the book

The book is in two parts. Part One addresses the programme directly. Chapter 1 introduces the context of the programme – why it is needed and why now. Chapter 2 is a very short chapter with practical advice for facilitators. In it I share some of the best learning I have gained from my own experience of presenting *Joining the Dots*, which can be adapted to suit the facilitator's own style and the needs of the group. Chapter 3 presents the five-week programme, week by week, in the form of a text that participants can use directly and a facilitator can use to present to participants.

Part Two details the theory and praxis of the programme. In Chapter 4 I describe the pedagogy – grounded in the General Directory for Catechesis and brought to life through the Shared Christian Praxis Approach (SCPA) of Thomas H. Groome. The final chapter delineates the theological conceptual framework and spiritual roots of the programme.

Acknowledgements

In one way, it is not difficult to trace the beginnings of *Joining the Dots*. John O'Roarke, Principal of Mercy Mounthawk, Tralee, set the challenge and collaborated on the initial venture; fifteen members of his staff took part in that pilot run of seven weeks. Their active participation, feedback and evaluation transformed the project. It would never have got off the ground if other schools had not taken the plunge – St Mary's Secondary School, Mallow; Coláiste na Toirbhirte, Bandon; St Mary's Secondary School, Nenagh; and Christ the King Secondary School, Cork were all early hosts.

My colleagues in ceist, especially Anne Kelleher CEO, Ned Prendergast, Director of Faith Development, Lloyd Bracken and Margaret Farrell, made it possible for me to take on this project and encouraged me all the way. Their understanding of the human spirit and its impact on education is rare and heartening. Margaret deserves enormous credit for taking the programme to Nenagh while it was still on scraps of paper! Thank you also to Maura Hyland, Donna Doherty and the team in Veritas. Donna's enthusiasm right from the start was effervescent.

The deeper roots of the programme can be traced to Coláiste Iognáid Galway where Terry Howard SJ, with an ancient text and his own exceptional skill, guided me through a spiritual journey which would change my life. Tom Groome and Boston College provided the project with an academic home. Under Tom's direction, BC's Institute of Religious Education and Pastoral Ministry (IREPM) showed me just how life-giving a Christian community can be, especially when it holds in balance all the ministries of the early Church.

In many ways my husband Dan O'Connell is the silent partner in this project. Without his help, the material for the programme would never have evolved, and he wrote the final chapter with me. The depth of his learning was invaluable. Of course his contribution went way beyond that – his belief in the wider project and his belief in me, his vitality, interest and constant good humour make everything a joy.

NOTES

1. Luke 10:38-42.
2. CEIST (Catholic Education, an Irish Schools Trust) is a new organisational framework for exercising educational trusteeship set up by the Daughters of Charity, the Presentation Sisters, the Sisters of the Christian Retreat, the Sisters of Mercy, and the Missionaries of the Sacred Heart. In existence since 2007, CEIST has responsibility for 110 schools associated with the five collaborating congregations in the Republic of Ireland. One of my first school visits as Faith Development Coordinator with CEIST was to Mercy Mounthawk in Tralee where the principal, John O'Roarke, engaged me in a conversation on the need to support teachers in Catholic schools.

Part 1

one Original Context:
The Irish Catholic School

It will not do to leave a ... dragon out of your plans
if you live near one.

(J.R.R. Tolkien, from *The Hobbit*)[1]

The nature of education

There is no doubt but that educating is a busy profession. Four months after his election in May 2007, president of France Nicolas Sarkozy wrote an open letter to French educators outlining his views and priorities. In it he acknowledged the primordial importance of the teacher's role and 'how demanding the marvellous career of a teacher is, how it forces you to give a lot of yourself, also how difficult and sometimes unrewarding it has become since violence entered schools.'[2]

Sarkozy may have been addressing a French audience, but his words and sentiment find echo across many Western states. Teaching has become a difficult profession, far beyond its inherent challenges. The problems of a society tend to be reflected in its schools; the school operates as a microcosm of society. A recent Organisation for Economic Cooperation and Development (OECD) report identifies problems such as image and profile of the job, public confidence in and affirmation of teachers' work, the quality of pre-service teacher education, the opportunities for continuing professional development, for partnership and input to policy, the conditions of work, opportunities for diversification and supports in times of difficulty. The report also admits further difficulties and problems among which are the lack of teacher induction systems, the unsatisfactory condition of some school buildings, inadequate investment in teaching resources and equipment, high pupil-teacher ratios, and the stress levels in some teaching contexts. Another problem, emerging from the policy of pupil integration, is the training of classroom teachers as well as learning support assistants for pupils with disabilities. When these factors are appraised, they reflect a complex, changing and challenging world of teaching.

In the face of these difficulties, one might wonder why teachers stay in the profession. American education researcher Sonia Nieto concludes that what keeps teachers going has largely to do with their inner lives. Nieto's findings resonate with an emergent body of literature which concludes that it is the inner spirit that makes and sustains good teachers.[3] Nourishing the spiritual lives of teachers is crucial; healthy spirituality can be a sustaining force, helping teachers to thrive rather than simply survive in our schools today. A teacher does not merely impart knowledge. A teacher is a mediator between the knower, the known and the would-be knower, between the learner and what is to be learned. A person, not some theory, is the living link in the epistemological chain. The way a teacher plays the role of mediator conveys both an epistemology and an ethic – an approach to knowing and an approach to living. If Parker Palmer is right when he says 'we teach who we are',[4] then now more than ever there is a need for intentionally engaging and nurturing the spirituality of teachers.

The Christian tradition

The Catholic Christian tradition is a rich resource for nourishing the spirituality of teachers in Catholic schools. Indeed it considers that, because 'the Catholic educator must be a source of spiritual inspiration … formation is indispensable … and must be kept up to date … and in harmony with human formation as a whole'.[5] Constant busyness and over-busyness of teachers' daily lives militates against nourishing their inner lives. However, research has shown that reflection on the experiences of daily life – the good and the bad – sustains our spirits. Despite the religious history of education in this country, there appear to be very few opportunities either in teacher preparation programmes or in continuous professional development for teachers to explore the spiritual dimension of the human person, or more specifically, and perhaps more importantly, of themselves.

The Catholic school context

While they share many characteristics with other schools, Catholic schools seek to reflect a distinctive vision of life based on the Gospel of Jesus Christ. According to the Irish Bishops' Pastoral Letter commonly known as *Vision 08*:

> The Gospel sees the world in which we live as God's creation. As human persons, we are made in God's image and destined for everlasting life with God. Life is a pilgrimage in the footsteps of Jesus, who is 'the Way, the Truth and the Life' (Jn 14:6).[6]

This implies the fullest possible human flourishing in this world and a hope for the world to come. Fullness of life with God makes sense of our whole human existence. Catholic education at any level is an education with room to address the fundamental questions about the meaning of life.

In a climate of growing secularism, Catholic schools are distinguished by faith in the transcendent mystery of God as the source of all that exists and as the meaning of human existence. This faith is not simply the subject matter of Religious Education but forms the foundation of all that is taught and learned and the horizon of all that takes place in the school. This not only offers our pupils a rich heritage of wisdom but also gives them stability, a framework of meaning and a sense of direction for their lives in a time of rapid and often confusing cultural and social change. Daniel O'Leary describes how, in the Catholic school, God is at the centre of the learning process and is the ultimate goal of the curriculum. Although it may be convenient to speak of the 'religious' curriculum in the Catholic school, as though these were separate and distinct, in reality the curriculum as a whole, and every part of it, is religious, since there is nothing which does not ultimately relate to God.

Catholic schools are marked by an expectation that pupils will grow in self-understanding, develop a language of prayer, celebrate the liturgy and experience everyday realities as sacramental signs of God working in the world. God is found in the bits and pieces of everyday life. The spontaneous Spirit of God is equally at home in the awkward, the giddy, the sullen, the world of iPods and iPads. A further expectation is that pupils learn to make sense of their experiences and respond appropriately.

Catholic education can never be reduced to a process by which the State seeks to produce good citizens, or provide productive contributors to the wealth of society, or enlighten students about the wonderful new knowledge science has acquired. All these are undoubtedly part of the process but education is always about more and is concerned with the whole person and the community to which they belong. Catholic schools aspire to be warmly participative communities.[7] A Catholic ethos is not a set of rules or prohibitions. Nor is it a list of boxes to be ticked. Rather, as Benedict XVI says, it is a 'positive option', based on the recognition of the dignity of the human person called to a loving relationship with God.

The challenges

The challenges to shaping an authentic Catholic ethos are often daunting. Incessant advertising teaches young people that the desire for happiness can be satisfied by the acquisition of consumer goods and transitory gratification. Education is often reduced to competition for points, to the transmission of skills whose only goal is a career. Pope Benedict presents us with a clear assessment of these challenges when he says:

> In a society where relativism has become a dogma, the light of truth is missing; indeed, it is considered dangerous and 'authoritarian' to speak of truth, and the end result is doubt about the goodness of life ... and in the validity of the relationships and commitments in which it consists.[8]

Catholic schools as mixed communities

As microcosms of society, Catholic schools are a mixture of practicing and non-practicing Catholics, as well as some from other faith traditions and none. This presents a challenge for schools to remain inclusive, welcoming, participative communities and at the same time proclaim clearly and courageously the essence of all that we do: the Christian life invites a personal lived relationship with Jesus Christ. That is the heart of our Catholic schools. The school can provide plenty of daily opportunities for building that personal relationship and to participate in the communal witness to a multitude of such relationships. This implies, at the very least, provision of faith development opportunities appropriate to educators. As developing spiritually is a lifelong journey, educators need continuous opportunities throughout their working lives to reflect on the spirituality of persons and foster their own developing spiritualities.

Inculturated faith

Christian witness at a time when many predict that the 'centre cannot hold' is very important for the well-being of society at large.[9] However, for Catholic education to remain relevant in this climate it must meet the challenge of inculturation; it must root itself in the distinctive and real features of contemporary culture. People are hungry for healthy spirituality. The human search for meaning is as prevalent as ever and resonates through popular culture, as indicated, for instance, by Oprah Winfrey's Book Club choices. One of her most popular choices of 2010 was *New York Times* bestseller *A New Earth: Awakening to Your Life's Purpose.* When the author of the book, Eckhart Tolle, partnered Oprah for a series of webinars based on the book, they attracted more than 11 million viewers.

Similar indications emerge from the extraordinary success of books like *Tuesdays with Morrie. Tuesdays with Morrie* is a non-fiction novel by US writer Mitch Albom, later adapted into a TV movie of the same name. In the book, Mitch recounts time spent with his 78-year-old sociology professor, Morrie Schwartz. When Mitch discovers that Morrie is dying, he flies to Boston to visit him. From then on he begins to meet with his old professor on a weekly basis. During these visits he becomes aware that not only is he rekindling an old friendship, but he is also tackling a much larger subject – the meaning of life. Before these visits, Mitch had been living in the fast lane. A famous Detroit sports writer, he had no time or inclination to focus on things that really matter. The Tuesdays spent with Morrie lead him to change his life and outlook completely. The book is still an international bestseller.

Another example of inculturated faith is more recent and closer to home. London band Mumford and Sons are a group of twenty-somethings who blasted onto the music scene after their performance at Glastonbury 2009. Their debut album *Sigh No More* has sold over 1 million copies. They won the ARIA Music Award for Most

Popular International Artist in 2010, and the Brit Award in 2011 for Best British Album. Marcus Mumford is typical of his generation, describing his lyrics as spiritual but not religious. 'We're not a Christian rock band as such, the album deals with dilemmas every man deals with in life ... Faith is ... real and something universal.'[10] 'It's one subject that can't be ignored.'[11]

Faith cannot be ignored. Throughout history and at its best, Catholic education has honoured both faith and reason so that people can live well, as well as make a living. The heart of such an education is encountered especially in response to the great questions of life: what is, could be and should be.[12]

NOTES

1. J.R.R. Tolkien, *The Hobbit*, Wisdom Quotes, http://www.wisdomquotes.com/quote/j-r-r-tolkien.html (accessed 6 December 2011).

2. Nicolas Sarkozy, 'A Letter to Educators: President Sarkozy Writes to French Teachers and Parents', http://www.ambafrance-uk.org/President-Sarkozy-writes-to-French.html (accessed 6 November 2007).

3. See, for instance, the work of Parker Palmer.

4. Parker J. Palmer, *The Courage to Teach: Exploring the Inner Landscape of a Teacher's Life* (San Francisco: Jossey-Bass, 1998), 1.

5. The Sacred Congregation for Catholic Education. Lay Catholics in Schools: Witnesses to Faith, n. 62, http://www.vatican.va/roman_curia/congregations/ccatheduc/documents/rc_con_ccatheduc_doc_19821015_lay-catholics_en.html (accessed 2 August 2011).

6. Irish Catholic Bishops' Conference, *Vision 08: A Vision for Catholic Education in Ireland* (Maynooth: Irish Catholic Bishops' Conference 2008), 2.

7. Ibid.

8. Benedict XVI, 'Address to the Participants in the Convention of the Diocese of Rome' (Rome, 2011).

9. John Coolohan, 'Church, State and Education in Contemporary Ireland: Some Perspectives', in *From Present to Future: Catholic Education in Ireland for the New Century,* Eithne Woulfe and James Cassin (eds), (Dublin: Veritas, 2006).

10. From an interview with Laura Barton, guardian.co.uk, Thursday, 11 February 2010.

11. http://fourfingerculture.com/2010/07/12/four-finger-inspirations-ii-mumford-and-sons-sigh-no-more/ (accessed 30 March 2011).

12. Thomas H. Groome, *Educating for Life: A Spiritual Vision for Every Teacher and Parent* (Allen, Texas: T. More, 1998).

two
Facilitating *Joining the Dots*

> *There is no need*
> *to run outside for better seeing ...*
> *rather abide at the centre of your being;*
> *for the more you leave it,*
> *the less you learn.*
> *Search your heart and see*
> *the way to do is to be.*[1]
>
> (Lao Tzu)

This section includes guidelines for running the programme and guiding participants through the content and closing prayer of each week. It also includes some overall suggestions for creating and holding a prayerful, attentive, learning environment where there is room for people to be themselves, to talk and laugh and share in a way that is real and honest.

Running the programme: timing, sequencing and structure

The programme runs for five weeks. Each week consists of a 90–120 minute session, with a minimum of 90 minutes required. This is a tight time frame and needs to be carefully managed, though without being excessively controlled. The pace needs to move steadily without a sense of being rushed in order to honour the pedagogy and theology, the 'beginning, middle and end' of each session.

I have learned that in schools, there is no ideal time to run a programme like this, particularly outside school hours. People have children, parents, partners and spouses to consider, as well as a host of other commitments. I normally offer a choice between late afternoon and evening, but consistently the majority of interested participants have opted for a time slot immediately after the formal work of the day concludes – usually around 4.00 p.m.

There appear to be three obvious slots in the school year to run the programme: immediately before or after the mid-term break in the first semester or early in the second semester. It is important to run the five weeks sequentially, with no break, in order to maintain momentum. Of course, this is the ideal. *Joining the Dots* can be adapted to suit the timetable of any school and the needs and preferences of any group.

Joining the Dots is, of course, invitational; it can only work if people are invited rather than expected to take part. The integrity of the group is of the utmost importance, and for that reason participants need to be there because they want to be and not as a result of coercion – subtle or overt. For the same reason it is important that participants are on time, switch off phones, participate with an open mind and heart, listen attentively, maintain the confidence of the group, and resist the temptation to 'fix' each other!

Preparing your materials for each week
Standard materials you will need include:

a. Something with which to play the music;
b. Materials with which to create a prayerful environment, especially candles;
c. A copy of the programme for every participant.

It is important that every participant has a copy of the programme so that they can engage personally with the poems, parables and particularly with the works of art. However, in order to honour the pedagogy, *participants should not take possession of the textbooks until towards the end of the programme* in Week 5. Therefore it is important that the facilitator distributes the text only on these occasions and gathers them immediately. A personal copy of the text is important in Week 5 to pull the programme together formally by recalling previous content and conversation. The text can also act as a starting point for participants, either as a group or individually, who wish to continue into the future.

Additional materials for each week:

Week 1
Music: Robbie Williams, 'Feel' (from the album *Escapology*)
Mozart, *Confutatis* (from Requiem Mass in D Minor (k.626))
Leonard Cohen, 'If It Be Your Will' feat. The Webb Sisters (from the album *Leonard Cohen Live in London*)

Week 2
Film: *Bruce Almighty*, Chapter 18
Drawing materials: at least two pages of blank white paper per person and a good selection of coloured drawing pencils

Week 3
Music: Cat Stevens, 'Morning Has Broken' (from the album *Teaser and The Firecat*)

Week 4
Music: Shaun Davey, 'The Deer's Cry' feat. Rita Connolly (from the album *The Pilgrim*)

Week 5
Music: Leonard Cohen, 'Anthem' (from the album *Leonard Cohen Live in London*)
Writing materials: Large board or chart and writing materials

Facilitators will need to make themselves very familiar beforehand with the content and structure of each week.

Facilitation by means of SCPA

It is important that the facilitator is familiar with the Shared Christian Praxis Approach (SCPA) of Thomas H. Groome.[*] This is a carefully thought-out pedagogy which requires particular disposition and abilities. SCPA stands or falls on the ability of the facilitator to manage time well, listen carefully, ask good questions

---

[*] Facilitators who wish to familiarise or refamiliarise themselves with SCPA should read Chapter 4, The Pedagogy of *Joining the Dots*, and Tom Groome's *Will There Be Faith?*, Chapters 8 and 9.

at appropriate times, ensure a balance of all voices are respectfully heard, and avoid the temptation to fill the silences. The wisdom of the group – regardless of the profile of the participants – is paramount.

From my own encounters with SCPA, I am also struck by the importance of pause, of intentional silence, especially for critical reflection. Noise, even easy chat, can be ambiguous. It can speak of ease and atmosphere, but it can also serve as a distraction. There can be something gently persuasive about a question that is intentionally met with silence – a dissonance that is both centring and challenging. As an initial response to any question, Groome encourages participants to write down their thoughts, to take a note to themselves. In that moment of silence, participants get a chance to reflect, to pull their thoughts and feelings together, and to enjoy the peace that can fall in the presence of quiet communal learning.

As with any pedagogy, the commitments that undergird SCPA are more important than the 'movements'. One of these is the need for the facilitator to intentionally engage the skills of listening; there is no need for input from the facilitator beyond the programme content. Another is the need to frequently step back and evaluate; there is room for improvement in every praxis. This requires reflecting back on the experience – what went well; what questions worked; what actively engaged participants' attention; what did they learn for themselves?

Facilitating group discussion and personal appropriation
In general, the only materials participants need to bring to class are a notebook and pencil. It is important that they know to bring these on the first day and every day thereafter, so mention this in your introduction before the session begins. The notebook has two main purposes – for participants to keep a record of their own thoughts and thought processing, and to facilitate group discussion.

Group discussion is an integral part of the pedagogy and intrinsic to the programme. *Joining the Dots* is very much about honouring the wisdom of the group, encouraging and enabling colleagues to share and hear each others' wisdom, and creating a community in which colleagues are comfortable and equipped with a certain level of language and conceptual understanding to do this well. It is also concerned with personal appropriation and decision-making. Discussion is essential to these twin elements, and to the SCPA on which the pedagogy depends. In order to honour this personal and communal understanding and appropriation, discussion is carefully structured. For illustration purposes here, I use the first question from Week 1: 'What sense do you get from this song?' After they have listened to the piece, I guide participants as follows:

a. *Take a moment to think about what you just heard* – what is your sense of the song, what message do you think it is trying to convey? What struck you/what did you feel as you listened to the piece? (Note: at this point keep away from names/proper nouns. Do not mention the author, performer or even the title of the song – here Robbie Williams singing 'Feel'. This may distract the participant from getting in touch with what the song evokes for them.)

b. *Make a note to yourself.* Write down whatever came into your head or heart. Do not censor. Do not judge your reaction. There are no right or wrong answers here. (Note: writing the reaction is important. It focuses the task and encourages everybody to come up with something. The 'no praise, no blame, no self-censorship or judgement' approach is one I learned doing the Spiritual Exercises. It is very freeing and allows for honest personal identification and analysis.)

c. *Share your reaction with a neighbour.* Groups of two are ideal. Because the time frame is tight, only a few minutes are given to this element of the discussion. If groups are any larger than two people, there is the likelihood that at least one person will not get a chance to share their reaction. During this time you can circulate between groups. Join a conversation and listen to what's said without prompting in any particular direction. This can be difficult! Remember, the idea is to lift up the wisdom that's already there, to make participants aware of the great resource they are to each other, and for participants to become comfortable about sharing something of themselves with each other.

Reassemble the larger group and take a cross section/snapshot of conversations. In a large group there is sometimes a sense of 'who goes first' and you can initially be met with silence. In that case, reframe the question; perhaps something like, 'I heard some lovely insights while I was circulating between groups that the larger group might like to hear.' Now hold the silence. If there is still no response, reframe it one last time (every invitation to conversation gets three chances!) and again wait. The temptation for the facilitator to fill the silence is often great – but don't give in. If there is still no response, don't get upset or hassled in any way. Some groups are very chatty; others take much longer to warm up. Thomas Merton advises: 'Love winter when the plant says nothing.'[2] Resist the temptation to fill the gap or give the 'right answer' yourself. Just calmly move on.

Negative reaction to a particular artist or performer

There are lots of songs, poems, pieces of art, music and literature sprinkled throughout the programme. All are carefully chosen for a specific pedagogical purpose – for instance, to help participants engage with the theme, reflect critically, or correlate life with faith. However, as many of these come from the world of popular culture, some participants may have a gut reaction to a piece before they engage with the context. For instance, in Week 1, if participants recognise the Robbie Williams piece, there can be an 'Oh no, not Robbie' reaction, or 'I'm a great Robbie fan!' reaction. Therefore before any piece, I introduce the author/composer/performer. (This is the only time I mention these details.) Then I ask participants to suspend judgement until they have heard it through: 'Forget about what you might know/like/dislike about the performer, just listen to the message and enter into the spirit of the piece.'

Facilitating a prayerful environment

It is vitally important that the programme takes place in a prayerful space. A prayer room that is well ventilated with natural light and windows that can open is perfect. If the venue is a more functional room, then a prayerful atmosphere can be made by:

a. Arranging the chairs in a circle.
b. Stacking remaining chairs and desks neatly out of the way.
c. Tidying up any bits and pieces left lying around or reminders of the activity that took place in the room during the day. For

instance, in a classroom ensure that chalkboards are wiped down, electronic equipment is turned off and flipcharts, whiteboards or other teaching aids are stored away.

d.   Creating a sacred space using candles, fabric, greenery, flowers, an icon and/or an image – something(s) that recalls the presence of God in a deliberate way and sets the space as peaceful and welcoming.

e.   Creating a sense of welcome and hospitality through your own early presence and honouring the precious resource that is people's time by starting punctually. In the same way, remain as an unhurried presence in the room as people leave. There should be no sense of hurry before, during or after any session.

The role of the principal/parish priest

From time to time I have been asked if it is necessary for the principal/ parish priest to take part in order for *Joining the Dots* to run or really catch on in a school or parish. The answer is that it is not necessary for the principal/priest to take an active role. What is necessary is that the community leader is fully on board and committed to the programme, not just as a once-off occurrence in the life of his/her leadership tenure, but as part of ongoing professional development for staff. *Joining the Dots* fits into a deliberate process of faith development emphasised by the Church. It will bear fruit only with ongoing commitment for which the support of the principal/parish priest is paramount.

Facilitating the group towards the next step

Whereas the programme concludes after Week 5, there is always a hope that the group might decide to continue in some shape or form. The conversation towards the end of Week 5 allows for this potential to be explored. However, it is very important that any decision to continue on as a group and the shape that might take comes from the group itself. A wish to continue to gather, to discuss, perhaps to read and explore spiritual, theological and catechetical texts, perhaps to pray, is not a foregone conclusion. There must be very real space for people to say, 'I enjoyed the programme, but that's enough for me' or indeed, 'I started the programme so I saw it through, but gathering like this or continuing as a group is not something that appeals to me.' On the other hand, the facilitator has an invaluable role if the group, or some members of it, decide that they want to continue; for instance, by offering guidance on content, process and structure as they self-direct for the future.

Preparing yourself for each session

Attentive listening, finely tuned pacing, encouraging and maintaining balanced participation and holding a prayerful environment are pivotal to *Joining the Dots*. The facilitator is there to honour the wisdom and experience of the group, to present the Christian story and vision, and to help personal appropriation, all in the milieu of prayer – sometimes formal, mostly informal. This is a challenging task and requires very careful preparation. This includes not only thorough preparation of content, materials, timing and pedagogy but also self-preparation. *Joining the Dots* is demanding of the facilitator's spirit. It is not something that can be facilitated in a harried state, with a perturbed soul, running between appointments, or at the end of a long and weary day.

Be sure to allow time and space for centring of self before each session. Different techniques work for different people. I have found that praying with the lectionary of the day, with the prayer form that will feature that week, or with a Scripture piece included in that session are all life-giving prayer forms appropriate to the task. Meditative chant can also work well here.

Nurturing your own spirituality

Finally, be mindful of your own spirit throughout. All good facilitators, like all good educators, need to pay attention to their own spiritual needs. Remember the old Latin adage, *nemo dat quod non habet*: you can't give what you don't have. Week 5 of the programme contains some suggestions on how to nurture your own spirituality.

NOTES

1. Lao Tzu, http://www.quotes.net/quote/3741 (accessed 6 December 2011).
2. Thomas Merton and Lynn Szabo, *In the Dark Before Dawn: New Selected Poems of Thomas Merton* (New York: New Directions, 2005), 99.

three

Joining the Dots – The Five Week Programme

WEEK 1:
Spirituality and the Journey of Life

This first week of *Joining the Dots* we explore the central nature of human spirituality and try to connect it with our work as educators. We identify our longing for God and God's longing for us, and explore how God has been revealing Godself to humankind throughout history and still today. Throughout, we reflect on the relevance for our own lives, especially our lives as educators.

Opening activity: We are Spiritual Beings
Listen to the words of this Robbie Williams song (or watch on YouTube):

Feel
Come on hold my hand
I wanna contact the living
Not sure I understand
This role I've been given

I sit and talk to God
And he just laughs at my plans
My head speaks a language
I don't understand

I just wanna feel real love
Feel the home that I live in
'Cause I got too much life
Running through my veins, going to waste

I don't wanna die
But I ain't keen on living either
Before I fall in love
I'm preparing to leave her
I scare myself to death
That's why I keep on running
Before I've arrived
I can see myself coming

I just wanna feel real love
Feel the home that I live in
'Cause I got too much life
Running through my veins, going to waste

And I need to feel
Real love
And a life ever after
I cannot give it up

I just wanna feel real love
Feel the home that I live in
I got too much love
Running through my veins, to go to waste

I just wanna feel real love
In a life ever after, there's a hole in my soul
You can see it in my face
It's a real big place

Group activity
- What sense do you get from the song?
- What do you think the singer is looking for?
- Make a list of your own deepest needs in life. Do you hear any echo here of what you are looking for?

The Longing of the Human Spirit

Language of 'the spirit' is present in many diverse traditions. Hasidic Jews talk about the spark of the divine in every being. Christians tend to use the term 'spirit', though there are some variations. For instance, Quakers refer to 'the inner teacher'; Thomas Merton (a Trappist monk) called it 'true self'. Secular writers use terms such as inner self, identity, integrity. What one calls it is of no real consequence, although we draw from our own Christian faith tradition and use the language of the spirit. What is most important is that one names it. This is crucial, because it is part of the reality of being human. It helps us to see ourselves, our colleagues, our students as more than raw material to be moulded to suit certain earthly ends. Despite our cultural bias that all power resides in the visible, outward world, history offers abundant evidence of the extraordinary powers of the human spirit and the impact it can have on our individual and collective lives.

It's strange, but have you noticed that when a need is met, you then want something else! Recall a time when you really desired something, perhaps a particular vacation, a promotion or even a pair of shoes! Remember the exhilaration when you got what you wanted, the great excitement and happiness at the time. But for some reason, this exhilaration doesn't last. At various stages in our lives, we want to be someone else, somewhere else; we want to know more, have more and feel more. At a fundamental level, human beings are always hungry, dissatisfied or restless. We are never completely and fully at peace in this life. There is always something nagging, something we long for. This longing can be for ourselves, for other people or for the planet.

> **Discuss together**
> - Can you identify with this sense of longing, of restlessness?
> - Do you think this restlessness is a good or a bad thing?
> - What do you think we are actually longing for?

Restlessness – a good thing?

Most of us try to silence our restlessness. There are healthy ways of doing so, like becoming our best selves, fulfilling commitments and responsibilities, developing our talents, and so on. But there are also unhealthy ways to respond. We might try to bury it through drugs or alcohol or give in to what we yearn for even when we know it is not good for us.

The great North African theologian Augustine of Hippo (354–430) says there is only one sure way to satisfy the deepest longings of our hearts. In his book *Confessions,* he writes, addressing God: 'You have made us for yourself alone, and our hearts are restless until they rest in thee.' For Augustine, our restlessness is a good thing. In fact, it is what makes us human. If we are faithful to it and respond appropriately, it draws us to God. We are not and never will be satisfied with anything less than God. So rather than think of our restlessness as a curse or a nuisance, Augustine sees it as a blessing. It can keep us from worshipping false idols – like fame or fortune, power or popularity. If we get to a place where we say that 'this' – be it work, idea, sport, experience, relationship, place, achievement, possession – gives me complete peace or makes me 100 per cent happy, that 'this' is all I need, then 'this', whatever it is, has become our 'god' – a false god, an idol. Augustine believed that our restlessness can prevent such a thing from happening. If we listen to the restlessness of our hearts, it can prevent us from settling for what is less than God, and can lead us onward to embrace God and live as People of God – the only true fulfilment.

As a deer longs for the flowing stream
So my soul longs for you, O God.
                              (Psalm 42:1)

Over to you ...
Does Augustine's proposal make sense to you? Why or why not?

Deep in our hearts we yearn for God, we want to be near God, at one with God. The French philosopher, Blaise Pascal (1623–62) put it another way when he said, 'There's a God-shaped hollow in the human heart that nothing else can fill.' Our longing for God is a holistic one – body and soul. This is something we know deep inside, and this knowledge surfaces during the journey of life, such as seminal moments when we are confronted by birth or death. Listen to Mozart's *Confutatis*. This movement, taken from his Requiem Mass in D Minor, was written as he was dying. Initially you will hear the confusion, almost terror, at approaching death, and then you will hear something quite different ...

Confutatis

Voca, voca me	Call, call me
voca me cum benedictus	call me among the blessed.

Mozart reached the same conclusion as Augustine and Pascal, although he expressed it in music rather than words. The greatest human longing is for God, to be with God. We strain deep inside to hear God's voice and want more than anything to be called by God, to be at one with God – part of God's loving community.

So this longing is resolved through relationship with God – allowing the Spirit to live and move and have its being in and through us. This is the real challenge because it requires a letting go. It takes enormous trust to hand over to God – to listen for God's will and to follow that plan rather than our own. Mary's response to Gabriel, 'Be it done unto me according to thy word' (Lk 1:38) is the great example.

When we learn to discern what God wants us to do and become the persons God wants us to be, then it is not our own ambitions, our own priorities, our own wants that drive us. This is difficult but not impossible. Human beings have been gifted with spiritual powers of the intellect and of the will – that is what equips us to make choices, for better or for worse. In other words, we have minds that are able to decide between right and wrong, and the free will to choose which path to follow. We live with the consequences of our choices. We sometimes make choices based on fear, on keeping up appearances, on anxiety or because we want control. Our best choices are made out of love. Life is a journey during which we must learn how to make such choices – to align our gifts of intellect and will with God's plan. This is why Jesus teaches us to pray: 'Our Father ... Thy will be done' (Mt 6:9-10). This is not something that anyone else can decide for us or impose on us. We need to learn how to discern and how to live the outcomes of our discernment. The Christian conviction tells us that when we learn to discern the will of God and live by it, then we will know peace.

Over to you ...
Listen to the Webb Sisters sing Leonard Cohen's 'If It Be Your Will' (he describes this piece as 'a prayer') to get a sense of what that might be like.

If It Be Your Will
If it be your will
That I speak no more
And my voice be still
As it was before
I will speak no more
I shall abide until
I am spoken for
If it be your will
If it be your will
That a voice be true
From this broken hill
I will sing to you
From this broken hill
All your praises they shall ring
If it be your will
To let me sing

Reflect and discuss
- What sense do you get from this song?
- How does it differ from the first song we heard? What makes the difference?
- What does it mean for you?

But on the other hand …
Up to now we have looked at the restlessness of the human person. But the other side of this is that God is all the time looking to connect with us. We are like two magnets, God and humanity, with a draw and a pull for one another.

Sistine Chapel Ceiling (1508-12): The Creation of Adam by Michelangelo (1475-1564). © Photos.com/Getty Images

God Reveals Godself to Us

Reflect and discuss
- What do you see in the painting, *The Creation of Adam*?
- What do you think it says about humanity (represented by Adam)?
- What do you think it says about God?

God wants to be in relationship with us

God wants to be in relationship with us, to communicate his own divine life to those he created and to adopt every person as his own son and daughter. This is what is meant by Divine Revelation: it is the constant action on God's part to become known to all humanity. God has been entering into this personal relationship with all humankind throughout history, is doing it now in our own lives, and will continue to do it until the end of time.

People have tried to describe their experience of this divine outreach through poetry, theology, art, music, literature and drama. It is humanity's experience and response to God's outreach to us that has given rise to religion, namely, living in relationship to God. (The English word 'religion' comes from a Latin word meaning 'to tie back to'.) For Christians, Divine Revelation began through God's action at the dawn of Creation, continued through his relationship with Noah, Abraham and Moses and the ancient Israelites, and reached its fullness in God's own Son, Jesus – God's Word made flesh who came and dwelled among us, full of grace of truth (read John 1:14-16).

An important aspect is that Revelation comes through an experience in which God freely reaches out to us and invites us to respond. Through Revelation we experience God's loving outreach with the gift of spiritual wisdom for our lives and the gift of grace to enable us to live it. While Jesus is the fullness of Revelation and there will be no Revelation after him, God continues to make himself and his loving plan of goodness known to us, and he will continue to do so until the end of time. Why? Because God never ceases to reach out to every person, inviting them into loving relationship and to live as the People of God. This invitation is to each person in their own particular situation and special circumstances. Whoever you are, wherever you live, however you feel – God is reaching out to you now and always.

From Scripture

The Hebrew Scriptures tell the stories of how God reached out to the Israelite people long ago and how they responded to God's invitation into relationship. It is from their reflection on and response to their experience of God's outreach that we get the first part of our Bible.

The Covenant was, and remains, a two-way agreement into which God and the Israelite people entered freely. God promised to care for the people and he asked them – just as he asks us – to love him by acknowledging that he alone is their God, and by caring for one another and for all the earth. As is the case in any meaningful relationship, there were some ground rules binding both sides in the relationship between God and the Israelites, many of which were taken for granted – things like fidelity, trust, support and respect. Such mutual agreements, or covenants, were quite common in biblical times. They were solemn agreements binding both partners, the seriousness of which was often sealed by a blood ritual (read Exodus 24:1-8). In biblical covenants, unlike legal contracts, it is the relationship between the two sides that is most important.

Here are some of the great covenants that we find in the Bible:

God made a covenant with Noah when the waters of the flood had receded. Among other things, God asked Noah and his people to have special care 'for human life' (Gen 9:5). God promised that 'never again shall there be a flood to destroy the earth' (Gen 9:11). As a sign of this covenant, God placed the rainbow in the sky (read the story in Genesis 9).

Later, God invited Abraham and Sarah and their descendants into a new covenant relationship. God promised Abraham and Sarah many descendants. They agreed that they would live as God's special people and their existence would bring a blessing for all the nations on the earth. The sign of this covenant was circumcision. (Read about this covenant in Genesis 12:1-4, Genesis 15:1-6 and Genesis 17.)

Later still, when God led the people of Israel out of slavery in Egypt, God invited them through Moses into a new covenant at Mount Sinai. Again, the great summary of God's invitation in this covenant was 'I will place my dwelling in your midst ... and will be your God and you shall be my people' (Lev 26:12-13). All the people agreed to live as God's own people and this time they received the Ten Commandments summarising the law of the covenant. The sign of this covenant was the law, the keeping of the commandments.

Then, in the fullness of time, God made 'a new and everlasting covenant' through Jesus, offering it to all humankind. Jesus ushered in the final and definitive covenant between God and humankind. The Israelites had often used blood as a way of 'sealing' their covenants with God. At the Last Supper, Jesus spoke most explicitly about 'the cup of my blood, the blood of the new and everlasting covenant'. In Jesus, God made this final new covenant – also called a 'testament' – with humankind. We participate in it by our baptism. The definitive sign of this new covenant is to love God by loving one's neighbour as oneself.

Talk it over ...

In your own words, can you explain:
- What is meant by divine revelation?
- What does the word 'covenant' mean?
- Why is God always reaching out to humanity?
- What does this mean for how you live your life?

How do we experience divine revelation today?

In Jesus, God became human. Jesus is now the human face of God to us. So, if we want to know what God is like, then we can look into the face of Jesus. In his person, in his teaching, in his way of relating to others and to the natural world, Jesus most clearly shows who God is, what God is like, what God is saying to us, and how we should live as a people of God. He said of himself, 'I am the way, the truth, and the life' (Jn 14:6). This is because he reveals the truth we need to know, the way we should live, and life that we can have here and hereafter as people of God.

Scripture and Tradition are always our primordial sources of God's revelation. However, we can also feel the presence of God when we experience something beautiful, someone loving, something precious, someone forgiving, something good, someone truthful. In our time, as from the dawn of history, God can be experienced in the people and the created world around us. In the depths of our own hearts, we can listen out for God's word in our lives today.

> **Over to you ...**
> *   Name an experience when you have felt the presence of God.
> *   How was that presence made 'known' (revealed) to you?
> *   How was God calling you to respond?

That which is written ...

Scripture literally means 'that which is written'. The Sacred Scriptures of the Church refer to texts that describe how people have experienced and understood the interaction of God with humanity and creation over thousands of years. These texts form one book called the Bible or Sacred Scripture.

There are two great sections to the Bible, the Hebrew and Christian Scriptures respectively. The Hebrew Scriptures that Christians share with Jewish brothers and sisters is made up of forty-six books. These writings are a storehouse of God's revelation to the Israelites, with great spiritual wisdom and guidance for our lives today. The New Testament contains twenty-seven books. Here we encounter again God's revelation in Jesus Christ, through his life, death and resurrection, and through the first Christian communities. Both Testaments were written under the inspiration of the Holy Spirit and are central to our Catholic faith.

The Scriptures are not just stories or information *about* God's interventions in human history and the response of peoples. They are also the inspired *word of God* to people today. God continues to speak to the world through the Bible. God's voice is alive and present in its texts, if we have ears and hearts to hear it.

To say that the Scriptures are inspired by God gives them great authority. They have a divine origin and God would never deceive us. St Paul wrote, 'All Scripture is inspired by God and is useful for teaching ...' (2 Tim 3:16).

So, the Scriptures reveal the presence and action of God in the world throughout time, and the great truths we can learn now from God's revelation. For instance, they tell us of God's power of creation, how God freed the people from slavery and led them into the Promised Land. They tell of God's constant desire to care for people and the responsibility – on the part of the people – that comes with such a covenant relationship. That God is our God and we must live as God's people is a central theme throughout all of the Scriptures. The Scriptures culminate in the telling of the life, death and resurrection of Jesus Christ. For Christians, the Four Gospels – Matthew, Mark, Luke and John – that record the Good News ('gospel') of Jesus are the heart of all the Scriptures.

Tradition

Tradition refers to the many ways the Church 'hands on' its faith to each new generation. It is through such things as preaching, witness, prayer and teaching that the faith is handed on. This is the large meaning – Tradition with a big 'T'. But there is also a more narrow meaning – tradition with a small 't'. This refers to the various Church traditions that have sprung up over time in various parts of the world. These are all expressions of Tradition. So, Tradition with a capital 'T' is the living and lived faith of the Church; and traditions, small 't', are the multiple ways in which this faith is put into practice by a particular people, in a particular place, at a particular time.

> *Tradition is the living faith of the dead, not the dead faith of the living.*
>
> (Jaroslav Pelikan)

Throughout history, men and women of all ages, times and places have struggled to live their Christian faith and to bring its wisdom to questions of life and death, of suffering and injustice, of meaning and happiness. Through their attempts to live authentically as disciples of Jesus and in the light of the gospels, they leave us a legacy of great wisdom – God's ongoing revelation – for our own lives. Tradition is not an imposition of someone else's truth upon us from the past but the offer of a rich treasury of tested wisdom for life. And when it comes to accessing this Tradition, from our own particular life situations, we must remember that Jesus promised us the Spirit of truth to guide his community: 'When the Spirit of truth comes, he will guide you into all the truth' (Jn 16:13). And the Risen Christ urged the disciples to 'remember, I am with you always, to the end of time' (Mt 28:20).

Together, Scripture and Tradition reveal God to us. They are the source of our faith. Our own experiences too allow us to glimpse something of God's divine plan for us and for our world. This faith, this Christian faith, is to be alive, vibrant, living and life-giving, for ourselves, others, society and the whole of creation.

The Courage to Meet God

This week has identified our need for God and how God is constantly revealing Godself to us throughout history. We can look in a special way to Scripture, to Tradition, and to our own experience to know and respond to God's outreach to us. We have talked about the longing of the human heart and framed it as the longing for unity with the divine. We know that God is always reaching out for us. 'My Father is still working and I also am working' (Jn 5:17). The Christian story/ vision traces this throughout time and into the future.

What about you?

What relevance has all of this for you? In other words, does the Christian understanding of our longing for God, God's longing for us and God's constant revelation have any meaning for your life?

Take some time to reflect. The following questions might help in the reflection process:

- Where do you see God in your work?
- What can help you recognise God in your every day?
- If you chose to build a relationship with God, how would you go about doing that?
- What have you learned today that might be helpful for your own life?

Sometimes it is difficult to hear the call of God or to know what God's will or plan might be for us. This is why prayer is so important. Prayer is the language of any healthy spirituality. During these five weeks, we will encounter many forms of prayer, most of which are age-old and have helped people communicate with God for generations. The first of these is the examination of conscience, also known as the examen.

Closing Prayer

St Ignatius of Loyola (1491–1556) was convinced that Christians can 'come to see God in all things' – if we are open and alert for God's presence. This is true for every aspect of living, including teaching and learning. The presence of God has been experienced as wonder, peace and joy, a source of life, a power that brings healing, forgiveness and hope. Indeed, through the ages, people have experienced God in all sorts of ways. Ignatius adapted an ancient prayer form to help people tune in to the presence of God in all things: the examen.

The examen

The examen is a very popular type of prayer that has worked well for people down through the centuries as a method for ordering their lives according to the promptings of the Holy Spirit. Once they get familiar with it, many people adopt it as an ongoing prayer habit. It is a powerful practice for allowing the Holy Spirit to work in our lives.

The examen invites us to look back on our day, focusing on feelings, on what moved us. Our constant attempt is to recognise how God's Spirit was moving in our lives and to discern how well we responded – so that we might be more likely to respond appropriately the next time. So, we reflect on gifts as well as gaffes. There is a place for judgement about things we did that may have been stupid, self-indulgent, cowardly or unfair. However, there is a bigger place for gratitude, for intimations of affection, and for the moments that lifted our hearts and helped us to sense God's closeness and the sweetness of being alive.

The examen is usually conducted at or towards the end of the day. It is generally modelled as a five-step process, taking about five to ten minutes as follows:

1. Quiet down and get comfortable; breathe deeply, becoming aware of your breathing. Recall that you are in the presence of God; thank God for the gift of the day.
   God, I believe that at this moment I am in your presence and you are loving me.

2. Ask for help from the Spirit to see the day as God saw it, especially to discern the highs and lows.
   God, you know my needs better than I know them. Give me your light and help as I review this day.

3. Review the day slowly, recognising the God-moments.
   God, help me to review the events of this day in order to recognise your blessings and my shortcomings.

4. Ask for pardon and give thanks.
   God, I ask your forgiveness for my failings and I thank you for all your blessings.

5. Resolve to listen to God's voice.
   As I look forward to the rest of this day, make me aware that you are with me; show me how to become the person you want me to be.

(Adapted from the outline used daily at St Louis University High School, where all students, faculty and staff dedicate two minutes of reflective silence to the Examen of Consciousness. See http://www.sluh.org/campus/pastoralministry/theexamenofconsciousness/)

Further Reading

Dorr, Donal, *Divine Energy: God Beyond Us, Within Us, Among Us*, Dublin: Gill and Macmillan, 1996. Chapter 1 – 'Where People Find God'.

Downey, Michael, *Understanding Christian Spirituality*, New York: Paulist Press, 1997. Chapter 1 – 'What is Christian Spirituality?'

Groome, Thomas H., *Educating for Life: A Spiritual Vision for Every Teacher and Parent*, Allen, Texas: T. More, 1998. Chapter 7 – 'A Spirituality for Everyone'.

Lane, Dermot A., *The Experience of God: An Invitation to Do Theology*, rev. ed., New York: Paulist Press, 2005. Chapter 2 – 'The Nature of Revelation.'

Lonsdale, David, *Eyes to See, Ears to Hear: An Introduction to Ignatian Spirituality*, Philip Sheldrake (ed.), Maryknoll, New York: Orbis, 2000.

Rolheiser, Ronald, *Seeking Spirituality: Guidelines for a Christian Spirituality for the Twenty-First Century*, London: Hodder & Stoughton, 1998. Part 1: The Situation, and Part 2: The Essential Outline for a Christian Spirituality.

Related Websites

Ignatian Spirituality: www.ignatianspirituality.com

Ronald Rolheiser homepage for up-to-date theological reflection: http://www.ronrolheiser.com/

The Examen of Consciousness: www.sluh.org/campus/pastoralministry/theexamenofconsciousness

WEEK 2:
Being a Reflective Practitioner in the Christian Tradition

Last week we explored our search for God and the Christian belief that God always has been and will always look for us. We concluded with a prayer form, the examen, that helps us to see God in all the bits and pieces of everyday life, including work life. This week we look to ourselves as educators and to Jesus – the Teacher of Christianity – to discern how we can be our best selves as educators.

To note: You will need additional materials this week: at least two pages of blank white paper per person and a good selection of coloured drawing pencils.

Opening activity: Reflective journaling
Think back over the last week. Walk yourself through the week – the classes you taught, the students you encountered, the colleagues you worked with, what you read or heard or saw. In your journal take a few minutes to reflect on this question: in the last week, where did you see God in your work?

Education as a Spiritual Activity
Listen to the following quotes and notice your gut reaction to each one. Spirituality is a very bodily thing. Our bodies communicate our spirits. Listen to the affect in you – the bodily spirit – as you hear each of these quotes. Remember there is no right or wrong reaction.

> *No other job in the world could possibly dispossess one so completely as this job of teaching. You could stand all day in a laundry, for instance, still in possession of your mind. But this teaching utterly obliterates you. It cuts right into your being: essentially, it takes over your spirit. It drags it out from where it would hide.*[1]
>
> (Sylvia Ashton-Warner)

> *A professor is one who talks in someone else's sleep.*[2]
>
> (W. H. Auden)

Every September is like Christmas, and every student, a surprise gift to open.[3]

(Mary Vassilikou Bicouvaris,
1989 United States Teacher of the Year)

Reflect and discuss
- What was your gut reaction to each quote?
- Do any of these quotes ring true?
- What is teaching for you?

Over to you ...
Think of a very good teaching moment. What were you doing? What was going on for you/for your students/in the classroom? Walk yourself through the memory of it. What image of yourself comes to mind? Draw it!

In pairs
Explain this image to a conversation partner. Now the conversation partner picks out the gifts and values it suggests to them and relays them back.

Parker Palmer, a great American educator and author of *The Courage to Teach*, writes this about himself:

> I am a teacher at heart, and there are moments in the classroom when I can hardly hold the joy. When my students and I discover uncharted territory to explore, when the pathway out of a thicket opens up before us, when our experience is illuminated by the lightning-life of the mind – then teaching is the finest work I know.

> But at other moments, the classroom is so lifeless or painful or confused – and I am so powerless to do anything about it – that my claim to be a teacher seems a transparent sham. The enemy is everywhere: in those students from some alien planet, in that subject I thought I knew, and in the personal pathology that keeps me earning my living this way.[4]

Discuss together
Does this description ring true? Why or why not?

He goes on to say that teaching, like any truly human activity, emerges from inside, for better or for worse. As we teach, we project the conditions of our souls onto our students and how we are together. Knowing our students and our subjects depends heavily on self-knowledge. If I do not know myself, I cannot know my students. I see them through a glass darkly, in the shadows of my own unexamined life. So to teach well, to be well, we must explore our own 'inner landscapes' and that requires three paths – intellectual, emotional and spiritual.

> By intellectual I mean the way we think about teaching and learning – the form and content of how people know and learn, of the nature of our students and our subjects. By emotional I mean the way we and our students feel as we teach and learn – feelings that can either enlarge or diminish the exchange between us. By spiritual I mean the diverse ways we answer the heart's longing to be connected with the largeness of life – a longing that animates love and work, especially the work called teaching.[5]

None of these three paths can be ignored. Reduce teaching to the intellect and it becomes a cold abstraction; reduce it to emotion and it becomes narcissistic; reduce it to the spiritual and it loses its anchor to the world.

From years of asking students to tell him about their good teachers, Palmer claims there is a secret hidden in plain sight: good teaching cannot be reduced to good technique, however masterful, although this is important. Good teaching comes from the authenticity of the teacher. When we come to know our own inner landscapes, the more at home we become with our own selves, and the more at home we become with each other and ultimately with God.

Reflect and discuss
- Do you agree with Parker Palmer's description of teaching as outlined in this piece?
- What struck you as you read it? What does this suggest?

Jesus as Educator

In the Christian Scriptures, Jesus receives and accepts the title 'Rabbi' (teacher) more frequently than any other title. (See, for example, Mt 8:19; Mk 12:14, 19; Lk 21:7; Jn 20:16.) On one notable occasion, he follows that acceptance with one of the most profound lessons on humility in Scripture:

> You call me Teacher and Lord, and you are right, for that is what I am. So if I, your Lord and Teacher, have washed your feet, you also ought to wash one another's feet. For I have set you an example, that you also should do as I have done to you.
>
> (Jn 13:13-15)

It seems that this 'example' of teacher as servant rather than status holder is what Jesus sees as a proper use of 'teacher'.

Jesus did not engage in a formal method of interpretation and instruction. Only the upper-class minority had the wealth and leisure to pursue learning in the formal schools of antiquity. The rest of society learned wise sayings from conversation or stories about the deeds of wise people. Despite the fact that every generation of disciples form schools of interpretation, Jesus has always remained the Teacher of Christianity. To get a sense of this extraordinary teacher, we look to the Gospel accounts of his life and ministry.

Characteristics of Jesus

Choose a Jesus story from the Gospel stories – one that you have heard recently, one that you know and love, or the first one that comes to mind.

- Write down what you can remember of the story.
- What does it tell you about Jesus as educator and what he values?
- What human characteristic of Jesus comes through?

As a group
Share your choice of 'Jesus Story' and the characteristic/value it suggests. As you listen to each others' selections, keep a record of the dominant Jesus characteristic each story suggests. At the end of the sharing process, recall the list of characteristics of Jesus that

came to the fore. In this way we build up a picture of the Teacher of Christianity. Your Scripture selections will lift up some if not all of the following Jesus characteristics and many others besides.

Forgiveness

One of the central values that Jesus preached was forgiveness. This comes through clearly in the story of the woman caught in adultery (Jn 8:1-11).

Jesus' forgiveness was unconditional, yet at the same time he challenges the woman to be her better self. 'Go your way, and from now on do not sin again' (Jn 8:10-11).

While Jesus requires forgiveness of us, this was a quality that was present in his own life. We see it in his extraordinary ability to forgive those who were putting him to death. This is the litmus test for Christians. Can we love our enemies? Jesus says, 'You have heard that it was said, "You shall love your neighbour and hate your enemy." But I say to you, Love your enemies and pray for those who persecute you' (Mt 5:43-44). This is a core value for Jesus.

> *It is easy enough to be friendly to one's friends. But to befriend the one who regards himself as your enemy is the quintessence of true religion. The other is mere business.*[6]
>
> (Gandhi)

Compassion

Another core value in the life of Jesus was his compassion for those in any kind of need.

- 'When he went ashore, he saw a great crowd; and he had compassion for them and cured their sick.' (Mt 14:14)
- 'He was moved with compassion by the situation and tears of the widow of Nain. "Do not weep," he said to her.' (Lk 7:13)

Compassion is the quality that allows us to deeply feel the suffering of another and act on the inclination to give aid or support. All through the gospels, even when the word is not explicitly used, we can feel the power of compassion at the heart of Jesus' life. Time and time again, Jesus is moved to help others.

Come to me, all you that are weary and carrying heavy burdens, and I will give you rest.

(Mt 11:28)

There are two dimensions to the compassion of Jesus. He noticed and was moved by the suffering of others *and* he acted to relieve this suffering. So to be a disciple of Jesus, it is not enough to feel sorry for someone without trying to help them.

Reflect and discuss
- Where do you see compassion at work in your education community?
- What sorts of things evoke compassion in you?
- What do you do about it?

Welcome and inclusion
In his public ministry, Jesus made a choice to reach out to those who were marginalised and excluded from society – public sinners, people who were sick and the poor, including unskilled labourers, people without work and those who begged.

Widows and orphans were often poor. They had no one to provide for them and in the time of Jesus it was very difficult for them to earn a living. The economically poor were totally dependent on others to provide for them. This was terribly humiliating. Status and respect were nearly more important than food or life itself in first-century Palestine. It was embarrassing to depend on the charity of others.

Those who are poor have always been prone to sickness and disease. In the time of Jesus, sickness was often seen as the result of possession by an evil spirit. Luke tells the story of a woman who was crippled, bent over and unable to stand up straight as being 'bound by Satan' (Lk 13:16). Sickness was also seen as punishment for sin – their own sin or the sin of a family member. A person's illness excluded them from membership of society.

Public sinners were treated as social outcasts. This class included people who had sinful or unclean professions: prostitutes, tax collectors, robbers, usurers (people who lent money and collected interest on the loan) and gamblers. Their lives put them outside the law.

These three groups – those who were poor, sick and public sinners – had one thing in common: they were all despised by wider society. They were seen as being lawless and immoral, consequently incapable of holiness and goodness; it was only right they should be pushed to the edge of society.

Jesus recognised the dignity in people who were poor, sick and sinful, a dignity that was eroded because of the culture of the day. Jesus' life claimed that God was opposed to the marginalisation of the poor. His actions revealed the love that God has for the weak, vulnerable and silenced. Jesus reached out to social outcasts in particular because he sought to *affirm* their dignity as daughters and sons of God. He did not give them their dignity. God had already done that. Jesus wanted to help them find it for themselves. In this way, he opposed anything and anyone that would undermine the inalienable dignity given to each person by God.

Reflect and discuss
- Who is marginalised in your school community? How does this manifest itself? Why are they marginalised?
- What are the implications of Jesus' attitude and relationship with the marginalised for our own humanity?
- What are the implications for you?

Friendship

We all value friends in life and Jesus was no different to us in this. In the Bible we see that Jesus had good friends, including Lazarus of Bethany and his two sisters, Mary and Martha (Jn 11:1-57). John's Gospel recounts an episode where Jesus receives word that his good friend, Lazarus, is dying.

But by the time Jesus arrives at Bethany, Lazarus has been dead for four days and his sisters are grief-stricken. And what is his response? He is deeply troubled (Jn 11:33); he is moved to tears (Jn 11:35).

Great sorrow and sadness in death indicates the presence of great love and affection during life. It seems reasonable to suppose that Lazarus and his sisters were great friends of Jesus. Jesus' friendship is close, supportive, yet challenging. We see this in his relations with his disciples – he constantly challenges them to be their best selves. This type of friendship is essential to our humanity.

Jesus as Son

Jesus was obviously close to his mother. He values her counsel and respects her expectations of him. This is beautifully illustrated in John's account of the Wedding at Cana (Jn 2:1-10). Although he tries to argue that it is not yet time, Jesus trusts her implicitly and bows to his mother's imperative 'Do what he asks'. There is a certain vulnerability about both of them in this simple exchange. Somehow she knows it is time for him to go, although that sword must have pierced her heart. Somehow he knows she is right, although the temptation to stay must have been very strong. Mary is present in Jerusalem in his final trial and stands at the foot of the cross. His last earthly thoughts are for her welfare – that his mother will be protected and provided for when he is gone.

Jesus' relationship with the Father is constant – prayer is a central part of his life. Quiet time alone in prayer is a central motif through all four gospels. For instance, Mark opens one passage with, 'In the morning, long before dawn, he got up, and left the house, and went off to a lonely place and prayed there' (1:35; cf. Lk 4:42). In Matthew we hear, 'After sending the crowds away he went up into the hills by himself to pray' (14:23). Time with his Father and time for others always hangs in the balance.

Reflect and discuss

- It has been said that the closer we get to divinity, the more human we become, and the more human we become, the closer we are to divinity. Do you agree?
- Close relationships need time and space and the ability to give of ourselves. The same was true of Jesus and it is true of our relationships today, including our relationship with God. Do you spend time with God? How do you pray?
- Why are family and friends so important?

The Challenging Jesus

The social context of first-century Palestine was structured hierarchically; every person knew exactly where they stood. The traditional clan and way of life would have been shocked by and reluctant to accept Jesus' break from ancestral ways of life. Almost everything about a person was determined by the place and patterns of relationship into which he or she was born. But Jesus was opposed to hierarchy. For instance, he continually advises his disciples not to 'lord it over' others, and in washing their feet at the Passover supper he demonstrates that to lead is to serve. Jesus broke with social mores in his dealings with women and challenges society through his forgiveness and miracles of healing.

Authenticity

We heard earlier Parker Palmer's conviction that 'good teaching comes from the authenticity of the teacher'. One of the characteristics of Jesus that resonates for educators is that he was real, he was authentic, he was himself. He did not try to flatter the crowd, impress the authorities, or ingratiate himself with the leaders of his day. We see this in his dealings with Mary Magdalene, Zacchaeus, those who confused law with love, even with Pontius Pilot.

One of the things that made him angry was the hypocrisy of others, especially those in power (see, for instance, Mt 23:23). They were too caught up in their outward appearance, their position in society, and protecting their own power. This prevented them from caring for the poor and helping people come closer to God.

Jesus taught his listeners the 'Good News' with authority, although he did not have the normal power systems or status to back up what he said. He successfully conveyed his message to groups of people through his integrity and personal appeal. Within Jesus there was a harmony between his inner and outer life. He walked the talk, so to speak, even when there was the risk of losing his friends, his reputation, his family, and his own life. He lived what he preached. Even his enemies acknowledged that he was honest and fearless: 'Teacher, we know that you are sincere, and show deference to no one; for you do not regard people with partiality, but teach the way of God in accordance with truth' (Mk 12:14). The authenticity of Jesus allowed him to teach with authority and integrity.

The Velveteen Rabbit[7]

'What is REAL?' asked the Rabbit one day, when they were lying side by side near the nursery fender, before Nana came to tidy the room. 'Does it mean having things that buzz inside you and a stick-out handle?'

'Real isn't how you are made,' said the Skin Horse. 'It's a thing that happens to you. When a child loves you for a long, long time, not just to play with, but REALLY loves you, then you become Real.'

'Does it hurt?' asked the Rabbit.

'Sometimes,' said the Skin Horse, for he was always truthful. 'When you are Real you don't mind being hurt.'

'Does it happen all at once, like being wound up,' he asked, 'or bit by bit?'

'It doesn't happen all at once,' said the Skin Horse. 'You become. It takes a long time. That's why it doesn't happen often to people who break easily, or have sharp edges, or who have to be carefully kept. Generally, by the time you are Real, most of your hair has been loved off, and your eyes drop out and you get loose in the joints and very shabby. But these things don't matter at all, because once you are Real you can't be ugly, except to people who don't understand.'

'I suppose *you* are real?' said the Rabbit. And then he wished he had not said it, for he thought the Skin Horse might be sensitive. But the Skin Horse only smiled.

'The Boy's Uncle made me Real,' he said. 'That was a great many years ago; but once you are Real you can't become unreal again. It lasts for always.'

The Rabbit sighed. He thought it would be a long time before this magic called Real happened to him. He longed to become Real, to know what it felt like; and yet the idea of growing shabby and losing his eyes and whiskers was rather sad. He wished that he could become it without these uncomfortable things happening to him.

> **Reflect and discuss**
> - Who is the most 'real' person you know? Describe why you consider them 'real'.
> - Is it possible for educators to be 'real'?
> - What makes it possible? What prevents it?

For Yourself – Discerning Your Native Gift and Values

At the beginning of our gathering today you drew an image to depict yourself when at your best as a teacher. Reflect on this image. Recall what you drew, how you explained it and what you heard reflected back to you about your image from your conversation partner.

- What gifts and values do you share with Jesus? How as educator might you put them to best use?
- What gifts and values would you like to share? What difference might they make to how you go about your work?

In light of this discernment, consider how it might make a difference to your work throughout the coming week – for example, how you see yourself, how you relate to others you work with, students and colleagues, or how you approach the subject you teach.

Take some time to write your reflections into your journal.

> *To thine own self be true, and it must follow, as the night the day, thou canst not then be false to any man.*[8]
>
> (William Shakespeare)

Closing Prayer

We conclude this week with a prayer form known as Contemplation of Scripture. It is a way of praying with the Scriptures and encountering Christ in them, through reflecting on his Word.

Contemplation of Scripture

There are a number of steps in the contemplation of Scripture:

- Become still
- Read or listen to a story or text from Scripture slowly

- Identify with one of the onlookers and describe the action to yourself from his or her point of view, as if it were unfolding in front of you. It might help to imagine you are reporting the story live for radio or television
- Read or listen to the story or text again
- Now insert yourself into the story. This time identify with one of the characters; walk in the shoes of that character. Mix, talk and become part of the scene. Be conscious of feelings, thoughts, imaginings and memories: what sounds, sights, smells, tastes, come to mind; what are you feeling; what are you thinking; do any memories from your own life well up?
- What is God saying to you through this story?
- Draw prayer to a close.

Now try contemplation of Scripture with the following Gospel passage (Lk 10:38-42):

Leader: Now as they went on their way, he entered a certain village, where a woman named Martha welcomed him into her home. She had a sister named Mary, who sat at the Lord's feet and listened to what he was saying.

But Martha was distracted by her many tasks; so she came to him and asked, 'Lord, do you not care that my sister has left me to do all the work by myself? Tell her then to help me.'

But the Lord answered her, 'Martha, Martha, you are worried and distracted by many things; there is need of only one thing. Mary has chosen the better part, which will not be taken away from her.'

Leader: Now listen to it a second time. This time place yourself in the scene. Be there when Jesus comes into town and knocks on the door. Participate in the drama as it unfolds.

Reflect
- Where were you in the drama?
- Who did you identify with most in the story?
- What does it say to you as educator?

Group discussion
What does this story and your experience of it as you entered into it say to you personally/as a group about your work in this educational setting?

Further Reading

Groome, Thomas H., *Educating for Life: A Spiritual Vision for Every Teacher and Parent*, Allen, Texas: T. More, 1998. Chapter 4 – 'A Community for Life', and Chapter 5 – 'A Tradition to Inherit'.

Johnson, Elizabeth A., *Consider Jesus: Waves of Renewal in Christology*, New York: Crossroad, 1990.

Nolan, Albert, *Jesus Today: A Spirituality of Radical Freedom*, Maryknoll, New York: Orbis Books, 2006.

Nolan, Albert, *Jesus Before Christianity*, 25th anniversary ed., Maryknoll, New York: Orbis Books, 2001.

Palmer, Parker J., 'Teaching with Heart and Soul: Reflections on Spirituality in Teacher Education', *Journal of Teacher Education* 54 (2003), 376–85.

Palmer, Parker J., *The Courage to Teach: Exploring the Inner Landscape of a Teacher's Life*, 1st ed., San Francisco: Jossey-Bass, 1998. Chapter 1 – 'The Heart of a Teacher: Identity and Integrity in Teaching'.

Treston, Kevin, *The Reflective Teacher*, Australia: Creation Enterprises, 2005.

NOTES

1. Sylvia Ashton-Warner, http://www.quotes.net/authors/Sylvia+Ashton-Warner%2c+Spinster (accessed 6 December 2011).
2. W. H. Auden, http://www.quotes.net/authors/Wystan+Hugh+Auden (accessed 6 December 2011).
3. Mary Vassilikou Bicouvaris, http://www.inspirationalquotes4u.com/inspirationalquoteteacher/index.html (accessed 6 December 2011).
4. Parker J. Palmer, *The Courage to Teach: Exploring the Inner Landscape of a Teacher's Life* (San Francisco: Jossey-Bass, 1998), 1.
5. Ibid., 4–5.
6. Mahatma Gandhi, http://quotationsbook.com/quote/16086/ (accessed 6 December 2011).
7. Margery Williams, *The Velveteen Rabbit*, Doubleday, http://digital.library.upenn.edu/women/williams/rabbit/rabbit.html (accessed 6 December 2011).
8. William Shakespeare, *Hamlet,* Act I, Scene III, http://www.enotes.com/shakespeare-quotes/thine-own-self-true (accessed 6 December 2011).

WEEK 3:
Imago Dei: Who Am I and Whose Am I?

This week we explore how being made in the image and likeness of God confers great dignity on every person and how human begins are made to be in healthy relationship. We reflect on some dominant images of God from Scripture, Hebrew and Christian, and on our own images of God, past and present.

Opening activity: Our Images of God

- Sit comfortably and close your eyes
- Breathe deeply and evenly
- Become aware of the silence and stillness around and within you
- Think back to when you were in primary school, about the time you were making your First Communion/Eucharist. Picture the classroom, the teacher, your friends. Remember your home. Where were you living, who lived there with you?
- Now call to mind your image of God from this time. How did you think of God? What/who was God for you?
- *Jot down your remembrances in your journal*
- Now think back to your senior year at second level. Picture the school, the teachers, your friends. Where were you living, who lived there with you?
- Call to mind your image of God from this time. How did you think of God? What/who was God for you?
- *Jot down your remembrances in your journal.*

> **Group discussion**
> With a neighbour, describe your images of God from your (a) childhood, and (b) as a teenager/young adult. Were the images similar or did they change as you moved from childhood into young adulthood? What do you think informed these images?

God the Creator

Listen to Cat Stevens sing 'Morning Has Broken'.

Morning has broken, like the first morning
Blackbird has spoken, like the first bird
Praise for the singing, praise for the morning
Praise for the springing fresh from the word

Sweet the rain's new fall, sunlit from heaven
Like the first dewfall, on the first grass
Praise for the sweetness of the wet garden
Sprung in completeness where his feet pass

Mine is the sunlight, mine is the morning
Born of the one light, Eden saw play
Praise with elation, praise every morning
God's recreation of the new day.

> Over to you ...
> What do you hear in this piece?
> What sense of God do you get from the piece? Explain your answer.

We heard in the first week of this programme that God is constantly revealing Godself to us. One way that people come to know the presence of God is through the mystery of creation. Oftentimes people relate their belief in transcendence to the 'wonderful world' they witness around them. Many cultures throughout the world tell creation stories. These stories reveal the beliefs of peoples about their origin, understanding of God and purpose in life.

There are often two main themes in creation stories. One is the origin of the universe and the other is the creation of features in the universe such as animals and human beings. Creation stories tell us how people understand God and their relationship to God.

The Hebrew Scriptures tell two creation stories: Genesis 1:1–2:4 and 2:5-24. The first one was written in the sixth century BCE when the people of Israel were in exile in Babylon. The second story was actually told first. It comes from a time and source nearly four hundred years earlier in the tenth century BCE.

The first creation story in the Scriptures tells of God's actions in creating the world and the second tells us about how God asked people to be stewards of creation.

First Creation story: Six days of Creation and the Sabbath (Gen 1:1-31)

'In the beginning when God created the heavens and the earth, the earth was a formless void and darkness covered the face of the deep, while a wind from God swept over the face of the waters' (Gen 1:1-2). This account goes on to give details of how the world came to be. Here is a summary of what it says:

Let there be light – the first day.

Let there be a dome in the midst of the waters and let it separate the waters from the waters – the second day.

Let the waters under the sky (dome) be gathered together into one place, and let dry land appear ... Let the earth put forward vegetation – the third day.

Let there be lights in the dome of the sky to separate the day from the night – the fourth day.

Let the waters bring forth swarms of living creatures and let birds fly above the earth across the dome of the sky – the fifth day.

Let the earth bring forth living creatures of every kind: cattle and creeping things and wild animals of the earth of every kind ... Let us make humankind in our image, according to our likeness – the sixth day.

'God saw everything that he had made, and indeed, it was very good' (Gen 1:31).

God rested on the seventh day.

Imago Dei: Image of God

> *And God created them in God's image;*
> *male and female God created them.*
>
> (Gen 1:27)

Imago Dei and dignity

Dignity is a deep word. It has something to do with the innate respect and ethical treatment due to every human being. The Book of Genesis tells us that we are created in the *Imago Dei* – the image and likeness of God. This is what confers us with dignity. This is the fundamental meaning of inherent human dignity – the conviction that every person is created in the likeness of God. Of course, the created world too has dignity.

Being created in the image and likeness of God confers great dignity and immense value on each person. On the afternoon of the sixth day, at the completion of creation, God looked at all of creation and saw that 'indeed, it was very good' (Gen 1:31). To be a person is to be *very* good! Our dignity does not depend on the colour of our skin, our achievements, our sexuality, our social status, our popularity, our reputation, our job, our ethnicity. No – it fundamentally rests on our identity as God's creation. If we are all created by God in the *Imago Dei*, then it follows that there is a basic equality between all people throughout the world.

The second creation story is very helpful in this regard.

The Garden of Eden (from Genesis 2)

In the second (but older)[1] creation story, we are told that while the world was not fully created, the Lord God formed an earth creature from the dust of the earth, and blew into the creature's nostrils the breath of life, and Adam became a living being.

Then the Lord God created the garden in Eden and placed Adam there to 'till it and keep it' (Gen 2:15). Then the Lord God created all sorts of creatures – cattle, animals in the field and birds of the air – and Adam named them all.

Adam is a Hebrew word which means 'taken from the earth', *adamah*. When the word *adam* is used here, it is usually translated as 'man', but more correctly it means 'earth creature'. This creature has no gender; it is neither male nor female and is not a man in the way we think of a man today.

The first creature shaped by God from the dust of the earth is genderless and alone.

The story goes on: 'It is not good that the earth creature should be alone; I will make a helper as partner.'

The earth creature becomes a person

Remember, the first creature shaped by God from the dust of the earth is genderless and alone. However, once 'the partner' is made, an interesting alteration occurs in the Hebrew text: it stops using the word *adam* (earth creature) and begins to use the word *ish*, which means a fully human male person. With the creation of the woman, the 'earth creature' becomes a man. Part of the problem for us is that in the English translation there is only one word used throughout, and that word is 'man'.

It is the creation of the woman that allows the man to become a person. In other words, while alone, the earth creature was simply that – a creature. Only in relationship, when a partner was created, could the earth creature become a person. The point is this: it is only in good relationships that we can be fully human persons.

The dignity of the person

The second creation story makes two very important points to do with the dignity of the human person:

- Men and women are of equal importance in the eyes of God
- Human beings are made to be in relationship.

Consequently, we must not think of dignity as something individual. We can only truly reach and live with dignity in the context of relationships and community. We cannot do it on our own. We are constantly connected to people and communities, near and far, living and dead. This connection is essential for living well. Week 2 outlined how important close relationships were to Jesus and how much of himself he invested in others. We are at our best when we acknowledge the importance of relationships in our lives; relationships that exist between us and God, others and the rest of creation.

Dignity undermined

There is so much in our culture and our world that undermines dignity and our perception of the dignity of others. We constantly receive messages about others – many of them mixed. Some of these messages communicate biases, telling us that some groups are less worthy of respect than others. These biases tell us to treat some with less respect than others because of their status, the colour of their skin, ethnic identity, lack of formal education, employment, personal achievement or social contribution.

Our response?

Perhaps nowhere else in Scripture is the power of God's word revealed more clearly than in the act of creation. Everything God imagined came into being through God's word. And God saw how good it was.

We have this same power; our words have the power to build up or tear down. Recall the times when you felt the effect of a harsh word on your self-belief or that of a kind word during a difficult day. By sharing in God's creative imagination we participate in the ongoing work of creation.

a. What strikes you about these stories?
b. What do they suggest for you as educator?

God the Loving Father

Among ancient religions, people believed that 'the gods' could be very ambivalent toward us, at one time loving and kind, at another hating and vengeful. Of course, this was their way of explaining both blessings and catastrophes; if the crop was good, the gods must be happy; if the crop was bad, the gods must be angry. So they constantly tried to placate the gods, to keep them happy – by whatever means they could imagine.

One of the great truths of divine revelation that began in the Old Testament is God's unconditional love for us. Even in the midst of suffering, whether by natural disaster or our own poor choices, God remains provident and loving toward us. For example, when Moses receives the Ten Commandments and returns to the camp with the two tablets on which they are written, the Israelites have already broken the covenant in his absence. Moses shatters the stone tablets but then reluctantly goes back up Mount Sinai on their behalf, expecting to encounter the wrath of God. Instead, in one of the great moments and texts of the people of ancient Israel, God speaks to Moses as follows: 'The Lord, the Lord, a God merciful and gracious, slow to anger, and abounding in steadfast love and faithfulness, keeping steadfast love for the thousandth generation' (Ex 34:6-7)

Jesus unveiled this revelation of God in its fullness by revealing God's unconditional love for all people. This is summarised in his constant reference to God as 'Father' and always as a loving father, calling us to live as his children.

Jesus teaches his disciples to pray to God as father (Mt 6:9), and God is referred to as Father in the Hebrew Scriptures many times:

- 'I was a father to the needy and championed the cause of the stranger' (Job 29:16)
- 'You are my Father, my God, and the Rock of my salvation!' (Ps 89:26).

Much of this image of God as Loving Father is summed up in the story of the prodigal son and his brother in Luke 15:11-32.

The prodigal son and his brother (Lk 15:11-32)

The story begins, 'Dad, why should I wait until you die before I get my inheritance? Give it to me now.' This is a shocking thing for any son to say to his father, and particularly at a time when it was very important to show respect for parents. Remember, of the Ten Commandments, the first four deal with our relationship with God. The first of the remaining commandments – which deal with our human relationships – refers not to priest, prophet or king, but to one's own parents. 'Honour thy father and mother' is the first rule in good human relationships. It is flagrantly broken by the younger son in Luke's parable. His demand for inheritance was also odd because the whole estate should go to his older brother. The demand made no sense. So what should the father have done? What would his hearers have expected? At least a good telling off! Instead we hear that the father divides up the estate and gives half to the younger son. This would have been a shocking turn of events to the people of Palestine at the time of Jesus.

Next the son goes off and spends the money on wine, women and song. But the good times don't last. A famine comes, and to keep himself alive he is forced to tend pigs. This is deeply ironic. Jewish people were forbidden to tend non-kosher animals such as pigs. However, things get so bad that the boy not only has to tend these non-kosher animals, but begins to envy them – seeking to fill his belly with the husks the pigs were eating. He has hit rock bottom.

At last the boy comes to his senses and says to himself, 'How many of my father's hired hands have bread enough and to spare, but here I am dying of hunger! I will get up and go to my father, and I will say to him, "Father, I have sinned against heaven and before you. I am no longer worthy to be called your son. Treat me as one of your hired hands"' (Lk 15:17-19). Notice, the reason for returning home is that he can eat well. There is no regret for how badly he treated his father or family.

The story tells us that the father sees the boy coming and runs out to meet him. When he reaches his son, he does not ask where he has been or what happened to the money. When the son begins the rehearsed speech, the father cuts across him, turns to his servants and commands them to get a ring, sandals and robe for his son and kill the fatted calf. He then takes the son into the house and the party begins.

There is no more mention of the younger son. But this story is not so much about the son as about the father, and it doesn't finish here.

Eventually, the elder son comes in, having worked in the fields all day. He is faithful and hard-working. He asks what is going on and is told it's a 'welcome home' party for his younger brother. He refuses to go in. In those days, refusal to share a meal with one's father was a very serious matter and to do so because of a fight with one's sibling would not have been sufficient reason. The father comes out to plead with him. This final conversation is what the whole story is about.

Remember, this story is being told to the scribes and Pharisees who have been complaining that Jesus eats with sinners and is willing to sit at table with them (Lk 15:1-3). The elder son complains bitterly to his father: 'I have worked for you faithfully and you have given me nothing, not as much as a young goat to have a party with my friends.'

The father answers, 'Son, you are always with me.' Everything he has is his son's, but 'we had to celebrate and rejoice, because this brother of yours was dead and has come to life; he was lost and has been found' (Lk 15:32). End of story.

This is a story about the incomparable love of and mystery of God as father. The older son complains that his father's behaviour is absurd and unfair. The father does not dispute this. These complaints are not important. The father is not as concerned with justice but with absolute, unconditional love.

The Pharisees thought they knew who God was, and how God acts. They believed in God as law-giver. God cares for the law, and if you step outside the law, then you step outside God. But for Jesus, no-one is outside the love of God. Even tax collectors and women working in prostitution are loved as much as those who keep the law; the sun shines on them just as much as on anyone else. God's love is faithful and eternal.

Reflect and discuss
- Which character do you relate to most in the story?
- What does this story tell us about God?

God's will for us

Jesus relates to God as loving father; the way he lives gives us a picture of who God is and what God wants or wills for humanity. God has a special will for justice and peace, love and freedom, for each one of us and all creation. We might think that we have made it in life if we are surrounded by money and possessions. But what God wills for us is so much more powerful and fulfils us deeply as human beings. Jesus makes known what God the Father wants for humanity.

Many names for God

We have spoken about God as Father, but we must be careful that the images we use for God do not foster or privilege men ahead of women or undermine the faith and spiritual power of women, or their identity as created in the image and likeness of God. The *Catechism of the Catholic Church* (*CCC*) is helpful on this point. To offset an over-reliance on male imagery, it says: 'God's parental tenderness can also be expressed by the image of motherhood' (*CCC*, n. 239). The *CCC* uses two biblical references in making this point. The first one is from the prophet Isaiah: 'As a mother comforts her child, so I will comfort you' (Is 66:13). The second is drawn from Psalm 131: 'But I have calmed and quieted my soul, like a weaned child with its mother' (Ps 131:2). The intimacy of maternal love reveals yet another dimension of God's love.

Reflect and discuss
What do you see in the picture on the next page?

Return of the Prodigal Son, c.1668-69 (oil on canvas) by Rembrandt van Rijn (1606-69). © Photos.com/Getty Images

Spiritual writer and theologian Ron Rolheiser explains that what the painting invites us to do is to see ourselves in each of the three characters – in the waywardness and selfishness of the younger son, in the bitterness and resentment of his brother, and in the forgiveness and compassion of the father/mother. Ultimately we are made to radiate both God's masculine fatherly and feminine motherly love. But before we can do that, we need to see ourselves, others and God with the eyes of God – to see with the heart.

So 'God' is not the name of a person – it is not a proper name. Nor is it the job description of someone 'out there' that directs what happens 'down here'. It is religious shorthand for 'absolute mystery'. God is the ultimate mystery that grounds and supports everything that exists. Up to this point, we have tried to describe God using metaphors: God as Creator and God as Loving Father. However, the fundamental metaphor in the Christian tradition, the least wrong way of talking about God, is God as love. This theme unifies all the Christian Scriptures and is laid out explicitly in the first letter of John (1 Jn 4:8, 16). It becomes the guide metaphor for all other metaphors.

God as *Agape*
Watch Chapter 18 from the movie *Bruce Almighty*.

In the clip, Bruce, who has been given the power of God, wants to give it back. It has become too much for him. In his distress, he kneels on a highway, praying to God, and ends up in heaven. Watch the clip to see what happens next.

Bruce Almighty (2003) –
Universal Pictures

God asks Bruce to identify what he really cares about. Bruce's answer is immediate and definite: he cares about Grace. Not Grace because of how she makes him feel, but Grace for Grace's own sake. What he really wants is for Grace to be happy. He wants her to meet someone who will see her as he does in that instant – through God's eyes.

Think it over ...
Bruce's love for Grace was not centred on himself. When God asked if he wanted her back, he replied, 'No, I want her to be happy, no matter what that means.' This is an example of *agape*, self-giving love. It is only concerned with the good of the other.

In his first letter, John uses the word *agape* for the love that is God (1 Jn 4:8, 16). This is a very peculiar Greek word. The normal word used in Scripture is *eros*, which denotes anything that seeks or finds satisfaction. So, for instance, to say I love that movie or I love playing golf – that is *eros*. A second Greek word used at this time was *philia*. *Philia* means friendship, brotherly love, the love of companionship (as in, for instance, the term 'philanthropy'). *Agape* was not a common word at that time. It denotes a love that is purely other-directed, that wants nothing in return, expects nothing back, not even gratitude. *Agape* is the pure and loving gift of self.

The great Johannine claim is that God is what happens between us when we love one another 'agapically'. The love that is God is love in the sense of self-gift. Love is a relationship and God is the ground of loving. This is the foundation of the mystery of the Trinity. Augustine used the terms 'Lover', 'Beloved' and the 'Love-in-Between' to describe the Father, Son and Spirit of the Trinity. This may be the clue to understanding the Trinity and what it means for our lives, now and always.

Reflect and discuss
- What do you think Bruce meant when he says about Grace, 'I want her to meet someone who will see her always as I do now, through your eyes'?
- What difference do you think it makes to see other people through the 'agapic' eyes of God?

What about you?
We know there are very many images and names for God; we have focused on God as Creator, God as loving parent and God as *agape*. We also know that God is mystery and no name or image can capture the fullness of God. We need to use many names and images to try to catch a glimpse or trace of who and what God is.

Closing Prayer

Our image of God can change depending on the stage and circumstances of our lives. What image of God resonates with you at this point in your life?

Symbolic meditation: Go out and meet God

Imagine you are sitting on a hill that overlooks a city. The sun is setting but the grass is still warm and dry. Inhale the scent of it and feel it under your hands and fingers. Feel the warmth of the evening sun on your face and the relaxing effect of the glow on your body.

You hear soft footsteps approaching you and you know it is an old hermit who lives in these parts. He comes to you and says gently, 'If you go down to the city this evening you will find God.' He turns and walks away.

You know in your depths that the man knows what he is talking about. Do you feel like acting on his statement and going down to the city, or would you rather stay where you are?

Whatever your inclination, imagine you now go down to the city to find God. As you rise and stretch, the city lights appear – a beautiful sight. They seem to be calling, welcoming you … What do you feel as you descend?

You have now come to the outskirts of the city. Where do you go in search of God? Follow the dictates of your heart. Don't be pulled by where you think you 'ought' to go or what you 'ought' to do. Just go where your heart tells you.

What happens when you arrive? … what do you find there? … what happens to you? … Do you find God? … or are you disappointed?

What do you do next? – do you choose to go somewhere else or do you just stay where you are? How do you feel?

Choose some image or symbol to represent what you found, what you encountered. Stand reverently before it. Speak to it. Now imagine the symbol speaks to you.

Stay for a while in silent contemplation. Then let go, but promise to return.

Come back to the room. When you are ready, open your eyes.

In your own space and by yourself, jot down or draw what you experienced.

Further Reading

Downey, Michael, *Altogether Gift: A Trinitarian Spirituality*, Maryknoll, New York: Orbis Books, 2000. Chapter 1 – 'Learning to Speak of God: Father, Son, Spirit'.

Gaillardetz, Richard R., *Transforming Our Days: Spirituality, Community, and Liturgy in a Technological Culture*, New York: Crossroad, 2000. Chapter 2 – 'The Life of Grace'.

Gula, Richard M., *The Good Life: Where Morality and Spirituality Converge*, New York: Paulist Press, 1999. Chapter 1 – 'What You Have Received as Gift, Give as Gift'.

Groome, Thomas H., *Educating for Life: A Spiritual Vision for Every Teacher and Parent*, Allen, Texas: T. More, 1998. Chapter 2 – 'A Good People'.

Himes, Michael J., *The Mystery of Faith: An Introduction to Catholicism*, Cincinnati, Ohio: St Anthony Messenger Press, 2004. Chapter 1 – 'Trinity'.

Himes, Michael J., and Donald P. McNeill, *Doing the Truth in Love: Conversations About God, Relationships, and Service*, New York: Paulist Press, 1995. Especially Chapter 1 – 'Exploring the Mystery of God in Relationships', and Chapter 3 – 'The Journey of Restlessness'.

Nouwen, Henri J. M., *The Return of the Prodigal Son: A Story of Homecoming*, New York: Continuum, 1995.

Shea, John J., *Finding God Again: Spirituality for Adults*, Lanham, Maryland: Rowman & Littlefield Publishers, 2005.

Suggested Websites

Australian Christian Meditation Community:
www.christianmeditationaustralia.org

The World Community for Christian Meditation: www.wccm.org

NOTE

1. Genesis 1 is a much later work from the sixth century BCE, whereas that of Genesis 2 is earlier, probably eighth century BCE.

WEEK 4:
Jesus – The Face of God

Last week we looked at our own images of God and some images that come to us through Scripture. As Christians, the most reliable reflection of God comes to us through the New Testament, which tells us that Jesus is the 'image of the invisible God' (Col 1:15). In Week 2 we explored through Gospel stories some of the many characteristics of Jesus that make him the truly human, truly divine person he was and still is today. Theologian Elizabeth Johnson describes how something 'incomparably good' happens to people in their encounter with Jesus Christ. They come to themselves, being restored to inner integrity. Relationships with self and others are healed and peace becomes a real possibility. Given the profound impact of Jesus Christ on our lives, the question arises – who is he? This question lies at the heart of Week 4.

Opening Activity: Jesus Today – Who Do People Say That I Am?

Given the profound impact of Jesus Christ in our lives, the question arises – who is he? The challenge for us is to decide for ourselves who/where is Jesus for us in our lives right now? This is the question at the heart of Mark's Gospel, the question that Jesus puts directly to his disciples:

> Jesus went on with his disciples to the villages of Caesarea Philippi; and on the way he asked his disciples, 'Who do people say that I am?' (Mk 8:27).

The second part of the question that Jesus asks his disciples is more difficult: 'But who do you say I am?' (Mk 8:29)

The Catholic Church has a long tradition of encouraging artists to express the Church's faith in artistic works. Indeed, the Church was the first great patron of the arts in the Western world. A picture can reach our imagination in a way that words cannot. Throughout history, great artists have shaped our understanding of Christian faith and in particular our image of Jesus.

Jesus of the People *by Janet McKenzie, 1999*

In 1999, the *National Catholic Reporter* sponsored a competition to see how artists saw Jesus. The editor at the time, Michael Farrell, wanted to see if Jesus was still of interest to artists as the new millennium approached. The competition attracted 1,678 entries from nineteen countries. Sister Wendy Beckett, the well-known art expert, chose the winning painting, entitled *Jesus of the People*, by a US artist named Janet McKenzie.

> Over to you ...
> Examine the picture closely. Spend some time looking at all aspects of it: the colours, the background, the clothes, the facial expression and any other details.
>
> Break into groups of two or three persons and share your impressions of the painting. The following questions might help to guide your discussion.

- Describe the picture in as much detail as possible
- Comment on the clothing
- Comment on the use of colour
- How would you describe the facial expression of Jesus?
- The artist used a female model for the picture: does this affect your response to it?
- What is your response to the artist's presentation of Jesus as a black person?
- What do you see in the background?

Now read what Michael Farrell had to say about it:

> It was, to say the least, controversial. The first thing most people noticed was that Jesus 2000 was black. Then the artist told the world she had used a young woman as model. The painting is basically what people call realistic or representational. I had frequently been asked what kind of image were we looking for. The point was not what we were looking for but what artists imagined.[1]

When you have reflected on the picture, answer this question:
• What is the relevance of this image of Jesus to your school community?

Jesus: A Reliable Reflection of God

God became fully a human being in Jesus. This central mystery is known as the Incarnation. Beginning with Adam and Eve and echoed throughout the ancient people of Israel, God had long promised to send a Messiah to save and redeem people from their sins, to enable us all to live as people of God. But that God sent God's own Son to be with us, as one of ourselves, was far beyond all expectations. In first-century Palestine, God took on human life in the body, mind and spirit of Jesus of Nazareth.

The 'Word' became Flesh

John begins his Gospel with the words, 'In the beginning was the Word, and the Word was with God, and the Word was God. He was in the beginning with God. All things came into being through him, and without him not one thing came into being' (Jn 1:1-2). This is the great summary statement of the Incarnation in the Gospel of John. We hear echoes here of the first creation story. There, 'God said' and things were created by the power of God's word. John's summary also makes clear that God's word was eternal and shared the same nature as God – in fact, 'the Word was God'. Then, twelve verses later, we hear the great punchline, the definitive moment in salvation history (the definitive covenant of Week 1): 'the Word became Flesh and lived among us, and we have seen his glory, the glory as of a father's only son, full of grace and truth' (Jn 1:14).

When we express belief in the Incarnation we are saying that the Son of God, or God the Son, embraced a human nature in order to bring us closer to God, to one another and to save and free us from the bondage of sin. Paul in his letter to the Philippians quotes a hymn that would have been widely known to the community there, some twenty years after the Jesus event:

Let the same mind be in you that was in Christ Jesus,
who, though he was in the form of God,
did not regard equality with God

as something to be exploited,
but emptied himself,
taking the form of a slave,
being born in human likeness.
And being found in human form,
he humbled himself
and became obedient to the point of death –
even death on a cross.

(Phil 2:5-8)

This is the heart of the Good News: that God came among us in Jesus Christ, to be 'like us in all things but sin', to show and enable us to live as children of God. Jesus Christ, who was born to a young Jewish woman called Mary and grew up in Nazareth in first-century Palestine, was truly God. This is what John means when he says, 'The Word was made flesh and dwelt among us' (Jn 1:14). In Jesus, God broke into the world and came among us as one of ourselves. What an amazing aspect of our Christian faith!

In your journal
- What does the phrase 'the Word of God became flesh' mean to you?
- Why is the Incarnation a central aspect of Christian faith?
- What is the 'best news' that you hear in this story of the Incarnation – for your own life now?

Mystery of the Incarnation: Emmanuel (God-is-with-us)
God is not human, but in order to save us, becomes human. The Incarnation, the birth of Christ is how God bridges the gap between the divine and us. Jesus is the love and tenderness of God, the means of friendship and the bridge between us and God. He is the way that God comes into our lives and draws us close. When Mary agreed to bear the Son of God she was playing an extraordinary part in God's plan to become human. Matthew tells us that all this took place to fulfil what had been spoken by the Lord though the prophet Isaiah:

Look, the virgin shall conceive and bear a son,
and they shall name him Emmanuel,
which means, 'God is with us'.

(Mt 1:23)

This is the central mystery of the Incarnation; God is with us in Jesus Christ. When we express belief in the Incarnation we are saying that the Son of God, or God the Son, took on a human nature in order to bring us closer to God, to one another, and save us from sin. This belief has been part of the Christian community since the life, death and resurrection of Jesus Christ.

This is the heart of the Good News; it is really what the gospels are all about. God sent his Son to be one of us, to be 'like us in all things but sin'. This is the Good News about Jesus Christ: although he was one of us, he is the Son of God. God has visited his people. He has fulfilled the promise he made to Abraham and his descendants. He acted far beyond all expectation – he has sent his own 'beloved Son' (Mk 1:1; cf. Lk 1:55).

> **Reflect and discuss**
> *When God comes among us, he doesn't first of all clear humanity out of the way so that he can take over; he becomes a human being. He doesn't force his way in to dominate and crush; he announces his arrival in the sharp, hungry cry of a newborn baby. He changes the world not by law and threat but by death and resurrection.*[2]
> (Rowan Williams, Archbishop of Canterbury)

Jesus arrived in this world as a newborn baby, dependent as all babies are on the people around him for food and water, love and support. Can you imagine Jesus as a baby, needing all the care and love that every baby needs?

- How does this image of Jesus as a baby compare to how you regularly think of him?
- What does it tell you about God and God's love for us?

The Why of the Incarnation

A Christmas Parable[3]

Once upon a time there was a man who looked upon Christmas as a lot of humbug. He wasn't a Scrooge. He was a kind and decent person, generous to his family, upright in all his dealings with other people. But he didn't believe all that stuff about Incarnation which the Churches proclaim at Christmas. And he was too honest to pretend that he did. 'I am truly sorry to distress you,' he told his wife, who was a faithful churchgoer. 'But I simply cannot understand this claim that God becomes a person. It doesn't make any sense to me.'

On Christmas Eve his wife and children went to church for the midnight service. He declined to accompany them. 'I'd feel like a hypocrite,' he explained. 'I'd rather stay at home. But I'll wait up for you.'

Shortly after his family drove away in the car, snow began to fall. He went to the window and watched the flurries getting heavier and heavier. 'If we must have Christmas,' he thought, 'it's nice to have a white one.' He went back to his chair by the fireside and began to read his newspaper. A few minutes later he was startled by a thudding sound. It was quickly followed by another, then another.

He thought that someone must be throwing snowballs at his living-room window. When he went to the front door to investigate, he found a flock of birds huddled miserably by the door. They had been caught in the storm and in a desperate search for shelter had tried to fly through his window. 'I can't let these poor creatures lie there and freeze,' he thought. 'But how can I help them?' Then he remembered the barn where the children's pony was stabled. It would provide a warm shelter.

He put on his coat and galoshes and tramped through the deepening snow to the barn. He opened the door wide and turned on a light. But the birds didn't come in. 'Food will lure them in,' he thought. So he hurried back to the house for breadcrumbs, which he sprinkled on the snow to make a trail into the barn. To his dismay, the birds ignored the breadcrumbs and continued to flop around helplessly in the snow. He tried shooing them into the barn by walking around and waving his arms. They scattered in every direction – except into the warm, lighted barn.

'They find me a strange and terrifying creature,' he said to himself, 'and I can't seem to think of any way to let them know they can trust me. If only I could be a bird myself for a few minutes, perhaps I could lead them to safety …'

Just at that moment the church bells began to ring. He stood silent for a while, listening to the bells pealing the glad tidings of Christmas. Then he sank to his knees in the snow. 'Now I understand,' he whispered. 'Now I see why You had to do it.'

> **Reflect and discuss**
> * What did the man mean when he said, 'Now I see why You had to do it'?
> * What does this story add to your understanding of the Christmas story?

Cur Deus homo: why did God become a person?

The very first Christians were totally convinced that Jesus' life, death and resurrection had made a fundamental change in our understanding of ourselves and how we can live. Yet how were they to describe this 'difference' that God had made in Jesus Christ? The first Christians began to ask it, and we've been asking and answering this question ever since. It is as if each generation must find the most forceful and effective language to 'tell the story' in its own time. One great theologian named Anselm (1033–1109) posed this age-old question as *'cur Deus homo'* – why did God become a person. Many opinions have been given, none the complete explanation since we are dealing with ultimate mystery.

> **Reflect and discuss**
> * Why do you think God became a person in Jesus?
> * What difference does Jesus Christ make in people's lives?
> * What difference does the Incarnation make for you?

The 'why' of the Incarnation from the *Catechism of the Catholic Church*

The *Catechism of the Catholic Church* outlines at least four reasons why God became human in Jesus and thus four consequences for us:

a. John's first letter tells us that humanity was in 'so miserable and unhappy a state' (1 Jn 4:9) that God was moved to visit human nature. In other words, the Son of God became human to bring us back to God – to reconcile us with God. This reason is summarised well every time we recite the Nicene Creed. We say that 'for us and for our salvation, he came down from heaven'. From the Latin *salvus* meaning to make safe or healthy, Jesus is the one who makes us safe from all powers of evil and brings us to good health as people of God.

b. So that we might really know the love of God for each and every one of us. The Incarnation tells us something about the nature of God. Through the Incarnation and then in the public life of Jesus we catch a glimpse of the extent of God's love.

c. To teach us how to live. Jesus models how to live as people of God and teaches us to do the same. He shows us how to live in right and loving relationship with God, other people, ourselves, and with God's creation. He asks his disciples to 'Love one another as I have loved you' (Jn 15:12). Not only does he teach us how to live, but he gives us the power to make it possible.

d. To make us realise that when we live like Jesus we are living as our best selves. At our best, we are closest to what is divine and we demonstrate to ourselves and to others the divine aspect of human nature. By living as our best selves, we reveal God's divinity to the world. This is an amazing statement, and yet if we remember the first stories of creation from Week 3 it should not surprise us. Made in the divine image, and alive by the divine breath, we are to grow in divinity. Of course we do this by living as disciples of Jesus.

So why did God become human in Jesus? We can summarise that Jesus, the Son of God, became human to save us by reconciling us with God, with others, with the world around us, and to empower us to become holy, which means to become our best and truest selves. He both reveals God's unconditional love and highlights our own potential. In other words, not only does he reveal God to us, he also reveals 'us to us' – who we can become – so that we might grow in divine likeness. When we live and love like Jesus, we move closer to the saving power of Jesus and to the divine potential within ourselves.

> **Reflect and discuss**
> There is an old saying that when we die, we will go before God. Rather than asking each of us, 'Why were you not more like Jesus?' God will ask, 'Why were you not more like yourself?'
>
> - What helps us to be our best selves?
> - What does it mean to say that in being our best selves, 'we might grow in divine likeness?' What does this mean for you, in your life right now?

The ongoing Incarnation

The risen Jesus appeared to many people, in many places, and at many times. Each time, something 'incomparably good' happened to the people who encountered him. Encounters with Jesus have continued down through the centuries. Whatever form they take, encounters with Jesus can have similar effects in our lives as they did for the first Christians. They bring peace, dispel fear, give us new hope, show us the deep meaning of the joyful and painful experiences we have endured, and fill us with the life and energy of Jesus Christ.

> *Christ has no body now on earth but yours,*
> *no hands but yours,*
> *no feet but yours.*
> *Yours are the eyes through which Christ's compassion must look out on the world.*
> *Yours are the feet with which he is to go about doing good.*
> *Yours are the hands with which he is to bless us now.*
>
> (St Teresa of Avila, 1515–82)

This might seem like an enormous responsibility. The world is so big and has so many problems. We need so much help and there are many others who need us. We need to remember that Jesus lives on in the world – this is the central message of the Incarnation. We are not alone. With the help of the Holy Spirit and the grace of God, we can be the head, hearts and hands of Jesus.

The most obvious way that Christians can encounter the Risen Christ is through the sacraments and the word of God through Scripture. Likewise, we encounter Christ thought the Church as a community of faith. On that hillside in Galilee the Risen Christ promised his little church assembled there, 'I am with you always until the end of the age' (Mt 28:20). Seeing, sensing and understanding the witness that Christians give Jesus can have a profound effect.

> **Reflect and discuss**
> - When you think of Jesus, what is human about him?; what is divine?
> - How best as educator can you participate in the ongoing Incarnation?

What About You: 'But Who Do You Say That I Am?'

> **For your journal**
> - How has your thinking about Jesus Christ changed or been challenged in light of this chapter?
> - What are the implications of what we have reflected upon today for your life/for your work as educator?

Closing Prayer
Responding to the presence of God
One of the ways to develop the capacity to recognise and respond to the presence of Christ in our lives is through prayer. As Christians, it is particularly important to focus on the events in Christ's life as found in the gospels when we pray.

One ancient form of prayer used by St Benedict about 500 CE is called *Lectio divina*, meaning divine reading. It is a way of praying with the Scriptures and encountering Christ in them, through reflecting on his Word.

There are four steps in the method:

1. *Lectio* (read): slowly read and listen to a passage of Scripture, paying attention to the words and phrases that strike you.

Lectio is a listening with the 'ear of your heart'. Reflect on the main ideas, images and people in the passage.

2. *Meditatio* (meditate): meditate on the words or passages that strike you. They are to be 'pondered in your heart'. Repeat the word or phrase that stands out over and over again to yourself. Allow it to speak to your head, heart and hands.

3. *Oratio* (pray): begin to pray to God. Speak to God from the words and/or phrases you were repeating earlier. What do you want to say to God? How do you feel, what do you remember? What do you hope for?

4. *Contemplatio* (contemplate): finally, begin to rest in the loving presence of God. There is no need to say anything, just rest and be present to God without words, listening to what God might be saying to you.

> **Over to you ...**
> Sit comfortably, breathe deeply and become still.
> Place yourself in the presence of God.

Leader: Jesus was travelling the road to Caesarea Philippi with his disciples. They must have been muttering among themselves about the identity of Jesus – and speculating on the rumours going around. Jesus asked them, 'Who do people say that I am?' The *National Catholic Reporter* competition shows that people today are still asking that question. As we pray the *lectio*, it is not the answer to the question that is important. Just listen with 'the ear of your heart' and allow the passage to speak to you.

Lectio: listen to this passage of Scripture, paying attention to the words and phrases that strike you. Reflect on the main ideas, images and people in the passage:

Jesus went on with his disciples to the villages of Caesarea Philippi; and on the way he asked his disciples, 'Who do people say that I am?' And they answered him, 'John the Baptist; and others, Elijah; and still others, one of the prophets.' He asked them, 'But who do you say that I am?'

(Mk 8:27-29)

Meditatio (meditate): meditate on the words or passages that strike you. They are to be 'pondered in your heart.' Repeat the word or phrase that stands out over and over again to yourself. Allow it to speak to your head, heart and hands.

Oratio (pray): begin to pray to God. Speak to God from the words and/or phrases you were repeating earlier. What do you want to say to God? How do you feel, what do you remember? What do you hope for?

Contemplatio (contemplate): finally, begin to rest in the loving presence of God. There is no need to say anything, just rest and be present to God without words, listening to what God might be saying to you.

Silently pray the Lord's Prayer.

To conclude

Listen to 'The Deer's Cry', preferably the version sung by Rita Connolly, which can be found on YouTube (the original old Irish text is also known as 'St Patrick's Breastplate'):

The Deer's Cry

I arise today
Through the strength of Heaven, Light of sun, Radiance of moon, Splendour of fire, Speed of lightning, Swiftness of wind, Depth of the sea, Stability of earth, Firmness of rock
I arise today
Through God's strength to pilot me, God's eye to look before me, God's wisdom to guide me, God's way to lie before me, God's shield to protect me
From all who shall wish me ill, afar and anear, Alone and in a multitude, Against every cruel, Merciless power, That may oppose my body and soul
Christ with me, Christ before me, Christ behind me, Christ in me, Christ beneath me, Christ above me, Christ on my right, Christ on my left, Christ when I lie down, Christ when I sit down, Christ when I arise, Christ to shield me, Christ in the heart of everyone who thinks of me, Christ in the mouth of everyone who speaks of me.
I arise today.

Further Reading

Dorr, Donal, *Divine Energy: God Beyond Us, Within Us, Among Us*, Dublin: Gill and Macmillan, 1996. Chapter 4 – 'Jesus, The Human One', and Chapter 5 – 'Redeemed by Jesus'.

Himes, Michael J., *The Mystery of Faith: An Introduction to Catholicism*, Cincinnati, Ohio: St Anthony Messenger Press, 2004. Chapter 3 – 'Incarnation'.

Palmer, Parker J., *Let Your Life Speak: Listening for the Voice of Vocation*, San Francisco: Jossey-Bass, 2000.

Rolheiser, Ronald, *Seeking Spirituality: Guidelines for a Christian Spirituality for the Twenty-First Century*, London: Hodder & Stoughton, 1998. Chapter 4 – 'The Concept of the Incarnation', and Chapter 5 – 'Consequences of the Incarnation for Spirituality'.

Related Websites

Lectio Divina: www.contemplativeoutreach.org

Lectio Divina: www.lectio-divina.org

www.prayerandspirituality.com

NOTES

1. From 'Christianity – Origins and Contemporary Expressions', Paula Goggin and Colette McCarthy-Dineen, in *Faith Seeking Understanding*, Micheál de Barra (ed.), (Dublin: Veritas, 2005), 22.
2. Rowan Williams, 'Sermon of the Week: Fear Not', *Alive-O* 8, Teacher's Book, Dublin: Veritas, 2004, p. 90.
3. Louis Cassels, 'A Christmas Parable', The Derry Diocese Catechetical Centre, http:/www.catecheticalcentre.org/index.php?pg=12&thought_id=18 (accessed 6 December 2011).

WEEK 5:
Connecting the Dots: Your Faith, Your Spirituality and Your Community

Last week we delved into the mystery of the Incarnation. God became one of us in Jesus Christ; we are now the ongoing body of Christ in the world. It is clear from his life and preaching that Jesus understood his mission as bringing about the Kingdom of God. As disciples we are called to do the same. The challenge of how best to do this within your own life and within your education community lies at the heart of Week 5.

Opening exercise: Ancient ministries at work in your school community

The early Christian Church realised that it should continue to carry on Jesus' mission. Within that mission early Christian communities discerned four particular ministries or tasks necessary in order to function as the Body of Christ in the world. The ancient Greek terms for these are summarised as:

- *koinonia*, meaning a credible community;
- *kerygma*, meaning word or message;
- *leitourgia*, meaning liturgy; and
- *diakonia*, meaning service to others.

They can be listed as ministries of *witness*, *word*, *worship* and *welfare*.

- Wherever the Body of Christ is gathered, it should be a welcoming and inclusive community that *witnesses to the faith* it preaches through its actions in the world, living as a community of Jesus' disciples in faith, hope and love
- Christian communities must always share, preach and teach the *Word of God* that comes through the Scriptures and Tradition
- The Body of Christ needs to *worship God*, offering the liturgy in a public way and as a community

- Finally, the Body of Christ needs to serve and promote the spiritual, emotional and physical *welfare of others* and the well-being of all creation.

> **Over to you ...**
> Divide into four groups. Each group will focus on one of the following ministries of the Church:
> - Witness
> - Word
> - Worship
> - Welfare

Think of all that goes on in your school community in any day, week, month and year. Now list the activities that represent your focus ministry at work.

In the large group, explain:
- How the ancient task you focused on is at work in your community today
- How you can further contribute to these task areas in your own community.

We were all baptised by one Spirit into one body – whether Jews or Greeks, slave or free – and we were all given the one Spirit to drink. Now you are the body of Christ.
(1 Cor 12:12-14, 17)

It is clear that to be the body of Christ, to carry on the mission of Jesus and the ministries involved, we need a community of people with whom to worship, bear witness, engage in welfare and interpret the Word. In short, we need a religion!

Spirituality and Religion
Do we need a religion?
Religion across the universe is communal; it is hard to believe on your own. Belonging to a particular religion is no guarantee of being a person of faith, even though that is the central aim of all religious traditions. Lots of 'religious' people would appear to be 'just going

through the motions' rather than striving to live their faith. At its best, a positive religion like Christianity can give people a profound sense of meaning and purpose in life, great hope in the face of difficulties, a sense of belonging to a community of care and support. A good religion can help to build unity in a fractured world, lend great spiritual wisdom for life learned over many generations, both living and dead. Religion at its best encourages people to flourish as fully alive people and to live their faith with integrity and honesty.

The universality of the golden rule in world religions[1]

Christianity	In everything, do to others as you would have them do to you; for this is the law and the prophets. *Matthew 7:12*
Confucianism	Do not do to others what you would not like yourself. Then there will be no resentment against you, either in the family or in the state. *Analects 12:2*
Buddhism	Hurt not others in ways that you yourself would find hurtful. *Udana-Varga 5,1*
Hinduism	This is the sum of duty; do naught onto others what you would not have them do unto you. *Mahabharata 5,1517*
Islam	No one of you is a believer until he desires for his brother that which he desires for himself. *Sunnah*
Judaism	What is hateful to you, do not do to your fellowman. This is the entire Law; all the rest is commentary. *Talmud, Shabbat 3id*
Taoism	Regard your neighbour's gain as your gain, and your neighbour's loss as your own loss. *Tai Shang Kan Yin P'ien*

Zoroastrianism   That nature alone is good which refrains from doing
to another whatsoever is not good for itself.
Dadisten-I-dinik 94,5

But religion is not always at its best. Indeed, there are times when
it seems that for too many, the outward show of religion is more
important than the inner life of faith. This can give rise to corruption,
empty rituals and people failing to live their faith in both their personal
and public lives. Religious tradition can be used as a mask in order to
gain the social standing that might follow from such a stance.

The shortcomings and scandals reflected at times in all religions
can lead people to go it alone, to cut themselves off from a religious
tradition and try to live their faith on their own. This is not easy
and is difficult to sustain over time. By stepping outside a religious
tradition, people can cut themselves off from the great spiritual
wisdom of that religious community which has been struggling with
the questions of life and death for thousands of years. Beginning
with the Book of Genesis, Scripture makes very clear that God made
us relational beings, to live together in community. Just as we need 'a
people' in order to emerge as a person and to live humanly, likewise
we need a community in order to live out the spiritual aspect of
ourselves. We are not so much human beings with a spiritual life
as we are spiritual beings with a human life. To live humanly and
spiritually, we need a faith community of true beliefs, inspiring
worship and life-giving values. We need a religion; spiritually, it just
isn't wise to 'go it alone'.

Spirituality and the sacramental imagination
As human activities, teaching and learning are spiritual endeavours,
ultimately grounded in a sense of the sacred. Having a sense
of the sacred as part and parcel of all that we do is known as
the sacramental imagination. Catholic celebration of the seven
sacraments – encountering God's presence and grace through
bread and wine, water and oil, and so on – encourages us to bring
a sacramental outlook to life in the world. With this outlook, it is
possible, as St Ignatius of Loyola proposed, 'to see God in all things'.
The poem 'Aurora Leigh' by Elizabeth Barrett Browning expresses
this beautifully:

Earth's crammed with heaven,
And every common bush afire with God:
But only he who sees, takes off his shoes,
The rest sit round it,
and pluck blackberries ...

Those with the eyes of faith and alert to God's continued presence in the world often find themselves like Moses at the burning bush (read the story in Exodus 3:1-12) – aware that they are on 'holy ground'. Many others, however, miss out on how 'earth's crammed with heaven' and just 'sit around'. The educator will always be searching for ways of revealing that this vague awareness of transcendence, this sensing of the divine in the midst, is already the work of the Spirit within each person – a Spirit that is somehow alive in the most ordinary experience, in the normal course of everyday life.

As the scenarios below suggest, there are times when as educators we have experienced something of the Spirit of the Risen Christ in our lives. Jesus was working in and through us, although we may not have recognised it at the time.

Read the list carefully:
- Have you ever forgiven a student, though you received no reward for it and that student took it for granted?
- Have you ever been good to someone from whom no echo of gratitude or comprehension came back?
- Have you ever made a sacrifice, without receiving thanks, without recognition, without even feeling satisfaction inside?
- Have you ever tried to treat a student with love when their behaviour was 'unlovable'?
- Have you ever persevered without bitterness in doing your best as a teacher when it felt like it was draining you of all energy, and/or left you envying those who have chosen a different career?
- Have you ever reached out to a student, not because you had to or else there would be some unpleasantness, but simply because of some mysterious, silent, unfathomable reality inside of yourself?

> **Reflect and discuss**
> - Have you had an experience similar to those listed above?
> - Why did you do what you did?
> - What gave you the strength to do it?
> - What difference did it make?

How are you doing? Your spirituality and your work

The scenarios above describe how the Spirit of God can work through us in the ordinary, informal encounters of any educational setting. However, awareness of how they can intentionally enhance the spiritual nature of formal day-to-day demands is also important to educators. They often ask 'how can I "evaluate" the spirituality of my formal work as an educator?' Theologian Michael Downey gives us a very useful framework within which to do just that. He reminds us that Christian spirituality is concerned with the Christian spiritual life as experienced by persons, in other words, with the Holy Spirit at work with the human spirit. This is done:

- Within a culture
- In relation to a tradition
- In light of contemporary events, hopes, sufferings and promises
- In remembrance of Jesus Christ
- In efforts to combine elements of action and contemplation
- With respect to charism and community
- As expressed and authenticated in praxis.

So for example, if we apply Downey's framework to a religious work of art such as Raphael's *Madonna del Cardellino* (see next page) we might ask:

- What was the culture within which this depiction of the Madonna was painted?
- What are the religious and theological traditions reflected and departed from in this painting?
- What were the significant events, hopes, sufferings and promises of the age in which it was painted? How does it reflect, nuance or critique them?
- What is the dominant image of Christ expressed in this picture?

(*questions continued on p. 93*)

Madonna of the Goldfinch *(Madonna del Cardellino) by Raphael (Raffaello Sanzio of Urbino, 1483–1520) c.1506 (oil on panel), Galleria degli Uffizi, Florence, Italy /The Bridgeman Art Library*

- What is the relationship between contemplation and action expressed in this painting?
- What is the understanding of charism and community?
- What forms of praxis result from such a depiction?

In the same way we can apply the framework to a Vatican document or an episcopal letter, or to any text, a piece of music, a stained-glass window, a school mission statement or faith development policy. It is more difficult when we apply it to our own work, because we are assessing an attitude or value system or faith life out of which we operate. But this is an excellent exercise and worth trying.

For your journal
Think back to a recent teaching learning experience that you led, perhaps a class that went well or a school event such as a liturgy.

Now ask yourself (jot down notes as you go):

- What was the culture of the group – age/learning ability/faith background/socio-economic background …
- What religious or theological traditions were reflected in the event or in how you conducted the event?
- How did the event reflect, nuance or critique the hopes, disappointments and significant events in the lives of your students/school community?
- What was the dominant image of Christ expressed?
- What action elements did it involve/what contemplative elements did it involve?
- What was the understanding of community expressed/how did it reflect the charism or characteristic/spirit of the school?
- What forms of praxis resulted from the event?

Reflect and discuss
- What was the best learning for you from this exercise?
- What would you do differently if you were to lead the same event again/what would you do the same?

As We Conclude the Programme

Best learning, challenges and opportunities

Ask God's Spirit for understanding as you review the learning that has emerged for you from *Joining the Dots*. Reflect back over the programme: in Week 1 we explored how we are longing for God and how God is always turned toward us, inviting each one into relationship; Week 2 lifted up the gifts and values you share with Jesus as well as those you would like to share; Week 3 highlighted the dignity of all persons – we are each made in the image and likeness of God; the Incarnation was the focal point of Week 4 – God became one of us in Jesus Christ and we are now Christ's body in the world.

> **Reflect/Discuss in pairs**
> What is the best learning that emerges for you:
> - For your own spirituality? Remember the quote from Parker Palmer, 'we teach who we are'
> - For your relationships with those you work with?
> - For the culture of your educational institution – for instance codes, policies, relationships with the local community ...

> **Reflect/Discuss in the large group**
> - What are the challenges to living out of a faith-informed spirituality? For instance, what are the challenges to being your best/real selves?
> - What in your work supports or endangers that spirituality?
> - How can you support each other through these challenges?
> - Where do you go from here?

Keep a spiral/circular diagram of your responses on a large board/chart during the course of the large group discussion.

Minding Your Precious Spiritual Self

1. The Catholic community as gift to our spiritual journeys

There are many ways and images used to describe the spiritual journey. Henri Nouwen talks of three movements: the first, from loneliness to solitude, focuses on the experience of our own selves. The second, from hostility to hospitality, refers to life as life for others. The final movement deals with the most mysterious relationship of all: our relationship with God.[2] The more we understand our own inner struggles, the more fully we will embrace a genuine life that is open to others and to God's will/plan for us and for the world. The ultimate goal is to say 'yes' to God – 'Thy will be done.' Discerning, trusting and acting on the will of God in our lives is an ongoing challenge. It takes personal commitment, and it needs communal support. In other words, we need, even and especially in the middle of our very real busyness, to make time and space for reflection and prayer – personal and communal. The gift of the Catholic school is that it makes room for all of this.

2. Creating time and space for the Spirit in a busy world

Leaving room for the Spirit in the hustle and bustle of everyday life and engaging in spiritual practices are paramount in cultivating a healthy spirituality. Here are some practical suggestions for doing just that. Not everything will appeal to everybody. The idea is to try them out as opportunities arise and then decide to integrate some – ideally one personal and one communal practice – into a regular habit. Then as time goes on or as your spirituality needs refreshing, re-visit the list.

- Commit to gathering with regularity. This does not have to be often; a realistic regular time frame is very helpful. For some groups this is monthly; other groups will choose to meet more or less often.
- Practice praying with Scripture, e.g. using Ignatian contemplation with Scripture, or praying the ancient method of *Lectio divina.*
- Experiment with the different methods of prayer active during the programme and choose one or two that appeal to you.

Engage in them daily. Digital media provide an excellent contemporary resource for prayer – personal and communal. Try the three-minute retreat from loyolapress.com.

- Walk alone with God. Although mountains, water and beautiful scenery are often considered most inspiring, you can walk alone with God anywhere. Leave the iPod at home!
- Commit to a pilgrimage, visiting a holy site or doing a retreat at least once a year.
- Participate in your local, life-giving Church.
- Find a spiritual director and engage with them regularly. Under their direction, consider doing the Ignatian Spiritual Exercises. Undertaking the Exercises is quite a commitment, but they have revolutionised the lives of so many.

In addition to prayer and attending honestly to our inner selves, we also need to engage in ritual with Word and Bread. We are sustained in community by gathering ritually around the Word of God and through the breaking of bread. This brings something that purely social gatherings cannot achieve: a transforming power beyond what we can rationally explain. Spiritual writer and theologian Ron Rolheiser advises that rituals are not exercises in creativity and should not be long. All great rituals are clear, predictable and short.[3]

There are thoughts which are prayers.
There are moments when,
whatever the posture of the body,
the soul is on its knees.

(Victor Hugo)

3. Advice for the long haul

Working as an educator can provide great food for the soul. What could be more life-giving than helping people to experience the 'breaking out' of God's own self, already and always present at the heart of the world. Engaging in the process of transformation and being transformed oneself in the process is indeed a privilege. But there are days when educating can be exhausting, draining, demoralising. Recall to mind Parker Palmer's words from Week 2. Remember – you cannot do it all. We stand on the shoulders of giants, accepting our own limitations, and we pray to God – loving parent, Son and Spirit to guide us to do what we can and trust in his Kingdom.

Finish by listening to a little of 'Anthem' by Leonard Cohen:

Anthem
The birds they sang at the break of day
'Start again', I heard them say
Don't dwell on what has passed away
Or what is yet to be

Ah, the wars they will be fought again
The holy dove, she will be caught again
Bought and sold and bought again
The dove is never free

Ring the bells that still can ring
Forget your perfect offering
There is a crack, a crack in everything
That's how the light gets in ...

Evaluation of the programme and its facilitation
Written evaluation of the content, process and outcomes of the programme – rigorous, honest and unidentified – is invited from all participants.

Closing Prayer Service
Gather in a circle, standing or seated, around a large candle.

Leader: (lighting the candle)
    Come Holy Spirit!
    Fill us with your love.
    Move us to bring your life to the world.

Leader: Gracious God, we give thanks for gathering us together these past five weeks and for the gift of each other. I invite each of you, if you wish, to share something you have learned for your faith, your work and/or your life, or an abiding memory from our time together.

Follow with a moment of silence.

Jesus, you called ordinary people to share in your work. Help us to hear and to respond to the prompting of the Spirit.

All: Come Holy Spirit, fill the hearts of your faithful.
Enkindle in us the fire of your love.
Send forth your Spirit, and we will be created,
and you will renew the face of the earth.
Amen.

Sign of the Cross

Further Reading

Groome, Thomas H., *What Makes Us Catholic: Eight Gifts for Life*, San Francisco: HarperSanFrancisco, 2002. Chapter 1 – 'What Stories to Tell? Interpreting Christian Faith', and Chapter 6 – 'In What Will We Invest – Risking the Leap of Faith'.

Irish Catholic Bishops' Conference, *Vision 08: A Vision for Catholic Education in Ireland*, Maynooth: Irish Catholic Bishops' Conference, 2008.

Kavanagh, Patrick, *Collected Poems*, Antoinette Quinn (ed.), London: Allen Lane, 2004.

McGrath, Alister, *The Christian Vision of God*, London: SPCK, 2008. Chapter 4 – 'The Holy Spirit'.

Metz, Johannes Baptist, *Poverty of Spirit*, New York: Paulist Press, 1998.

O'Leary, Daniel J., *Begin with the Heart: Recovering the Sacramental Vision*, Dublin: Columba Press, 2008. Chapter 2 – 'Restoring the Sacramental Vision: "Something Prevented them from Recognising Him"'.

Nouwen, Henri J. M., *Reaching Out: The Three Movements of the Spiritual Life*, New York: Doubleday, 1975.

Rolheiser, Ronald, *Seeking Spirituality: Guidelines for a Christian Spirituality for the Twenty-First Century*, London: Hodder & Stoughton, 1998, Chapter 10 – 'Sustaining Ourselves in the Spiritual Life'.

Schneiders, Sandra, 'Religion and Spirituality: Strangers, Rivals or Partners?', *The Santa Clara Lectures* 6, no. 2 (2000): 1–26. Available at: http://www.liturgy.co.nz/spirituality/reflections_assets/schneiders.pdf

NOTES

1. 'The Universality of the Golden Rule in World Religions', http://www.teachingvalues.com/goldenrule.html (accessed 6 December 2011).

2. Henri J. M. Nouwen, *Reaching Out: The Three Movements of the Spiritual Life* (New York: Doubleday, 1975).

3. Ronald Rolheiser, *Seeking Spirituality: Guidelines for a Christian Spirituality for the Twenty-First Century* (London: Hodder & Stoughton, 1998), 218–24.

Part 2

four
The Pedagogy of *Joining the Dots*

The art of teaching is the art of liberating people into an enduring possession of who they already are.[1]

(Daniel O'Leary)

If catechesis is about forming faith identity, then *Joining the Dots* is a catechetical programme. The intent of catechesis is to put people 'in communion and intimacy with Jesus Christ'.[2] It wants to 'apprentice' students to Jesus, promoting 'full and sincere adherence to his person and the decision to walk in his footsteps'.[3] Chapter 1 outlined the goal of Catholic education as a personal, lived relationship with Jesus Christ. So catechesis, as a subset of Catholic education, is a worthy focus. Of course there are different types of catechesis; not all catechetical approaches are the same. *Joining the Dots*, in line with the *General Directory of Catechesis (GDC)*,[4] calls for a catechesis that informs in Catholic Christian faith, helps form people to follow the way of Jesus in everyday life, and ultimately transforms both educator and student in the process. For this reason, it is probably more accurate to describe the pedagogy of *Joining the Dots* as that of catechetical education, which emphasises the importance of both catechesis: forming faith identity, and religious education: study of Catholic faith.

The process of catechetical education

The Second Vatican Council (1962–65) lamented the dichotomy between the faith which many profess and their daily lives, and declared it 'one of the gravest errors of our time'.[5] However, another serious emergent challenge is a falling away from faith. In other words, rather than living other to the faith they profess, many who were born into Catholic Christianity no longer 'profess' that faith at all. For instance, a recent Pew survey reports that one out of every ten adult Americans is a lapsed Catholic.[6] Further, many of those who stay have little or no engagement with catechetics or religious education after primary school and indeed are still operating from their 'First Communion faith'. When it comes to making sense of life, they sense its inadequacy.

The *GDC* echoes many times the challenge of integrating Christian faith and everyday life. But what if the Christian faith is long forgotten? The implications for the person and a community that has lost its memory, its sense of self are profound. If a community holds no other model of church than that of institution, if the tenets of Christian faith are presented as a list of rules and prohibitions, if some in the top echelons are seen to break these rules and accept little responsibility for the consequences, especially for peoples' lives, what draw or attraction does the community of disciples now hold? Because there is nothing surer: if faith is something one 'ought' to have – a duty rather than a life-giving encounter – then it has no future. During the most recent Irish census (2011), a lot of media commentary focused on one question – how many people would self-identify as Roman Catholic? What the question really seemed to ask was how one can identify as Catholic if the institutional Church has let them down? The process of catechetical education must therefore recognise the myriad starting points in any group; that the journey of faith is not linear and that it encounters many hurdles, some insurmountable, even for once-committed Christians.

The pedagogy of catechetical education
Education is the awakening and articulating of what is already in the human heart by virtue of the already graced nature of all creation. It is about deepening the perception of people who seek a richer understanding of what is happening in their lives and in the world. The pattern of beginning with the exploration of the human condition, of then revealing its potential transformation in the Incarnation, and finally of sustaining and celebrating this new creation is characteristic of Christian catechetical education. 'The experience of self is the condition which makes it possible to experience God,' says Karl Rahner.[7]

The *GDC* clearly favours a pedagogy that correlates the 'human experiences' of students with the great truths of Christian faith. Correlating life and faith is important to bridge the gap between the

Christian message and one's own personal and cultural context.[8] It also sees experience as 'a necessary medium for exploring and assimilating the truths which constitute the objective content of Revelation'.[9] *Joining the Dots* honours a catechetical pedagogy; it asks participants to interpret and illuminate their own experience with the data of faith. Interaction between human experiences – everyday and profound – and the revealed message is at the heart of the programme.

Thus, an appropriate catechetical pedagogy is one that:

1. Engages or promotes people's interests – with attention to their own lives. However, it goes beyond that to help them to:
2. Reflect critically on and learn from their lives in the world;
3. Pay attention to and come to understand thoroughly the content of Christian faith;
4. Make judgements, correlating and integrating their 'lives' and 'Faith';
5. Reach decisions – cognitive, affective, or behavioural – regarding life/Faith.

Such a pedagogy also reflects the 'dynamics of knowing' outlined by Bernard Lonergan: paying attention to data, reaching understanding, coming to judgements and making decisions. It also provides for critical correlation as a method of doing theology well.[10]

The pedagogy of *Joining the Dots* as one that honours all five of these challenges or 'movements' is the Shared Christian Praxis Approach (hereafter SCPA) of Thomas H. Groome. The aim of SCPA is to enable students to bring their *lives to Christian faith* and to bring *Christian faith to their lives* with the intended 'learning outcome' of *lived Christian faith*.[11] Groome describes his pedagogy – *from life to Faith to life* – as essentially a mode of evangelisation. Moving beyond the 'old' evangelisation which emphasised 'bringing them in' (bringing into the Church anyone not yet Catholic), the 'new' evangelisation emphasises 'bringing Christians out' – into the world with a living faith. Thus, the goal of evangelisation is to live one's faith with enthusiasm in every arena of life, to be joyful and living witnesses to Catholic Faith.

SCPA is particularly suited to the programme for two further reasons:

a. It is adaptable to any educational setting. For Groome, Catholicism is a spirituality (which he defines concisely as 'faith at work'); a God consciousness 'for the life of the world' (Jn 6:51). It can provide rich and life-giving foundations for any educator in the home, school and parish, and of any subject matter or discipline. The rich and life-giving foundation it provides is evident in the way we imagine great questions of life; what it is, could be and should be.

b. It is suitable for any educator. The heart of Catholic education is the spirituality of the educator. SCPA involves putting the faith of educators to work throughout the curriculum, through what, how, why and where they teach – sustained by the deep water of Catholic Christianity. Throughout history and at its best, Catholic education has always been 'educating for life'. Educating for life applies to every arena and on every level of existence; for one's own integrity, for the life of others, and for the integrity of all creation. It is for here and hereafter – God's reign of fullness of life 'on earth as it is in heaven'. It opposes what destroys or diminishes and fosters what enhances and empowers life. St Irenaeus, the great second-century theologian, expressed this essence of Christianity thus: 'The glory of God is the human person fully alive.'

Shared Christian Praxis Approach[12]
In his seminal work, *Sharing Faith*, Groome outlines his pedagogical creed as a Christian religious educator (although he further delineates this creed in his subsequent works *Educating for Life* and *Will There Be Faith?*).[13] The three articles of the pedagogy he describes provide a useful framework for reflecting on the aspects of human nature that, even in this post-modern society, we can consider common to all human beings. Groome sees the person as agent-subject in relationship – as partner in community, with the freedom, rights and responsibilities that inevitably flow from being made in the image and likeness of God. He views persons as communal subjects in right and loving relationship, conscious of our destiny to return to

the source from which we came. His third article refers to the person as both capable of sin and grace, with a reliable sense of right and wrong, yet ultimately in covenant with God.

Groome goes on to relate these articles with their pastoral consequences for Christian religious educators. Our proclivity for sin demands a pedagogy that identifies the sources and consequences of sin, yet reflects a profound confidence in the personal good of all participants in the learning process. The task of educators is to 'actively engage people's whole "being" in place and time ... and enable them to reclaim their past, embrace their present, and take responsibility for their own and others' future'.[14]

SCPA is an intentional 'way of being with' people. It is an approach for educators that realises both sound principles and effective practice. He calls it an approach because it is neither a theory nor a method exclusively; it is a reflective mode of going about the historical task of Christian education (which includes pastoral ministry). The term 'shared' reflects its participative and dialogical style; it engages people in a partnership of common reflection and discernment based on their present praxis and Christian Story/Vision.[15] It is Christian in the sense that it makes accessible the Story/Vision of Christian community over time and enables people to appropriate it in their lives. He refers to it as a *praxis*, which infers that we both intend what we are doing and can learn from it. It is neither abstract theory nor technical know-how. The term 'praxis' highlights that to learn from life we need to reflect on it with discernment, using reason, memory and imagination. It is reflective and informed, yet the intent is to put learning and insights to work toward good and practical ends.[16]

Groome's SCPA emerges out of a conviction that by reflecting on present praxis, that is, their lives in the world, a pedagogy emerges that engages the whole 'being' of participants as agent-subjects in place and time and the consciousness that emerges from their historical 'being'. This means bringing people to reflect on whatever is being done by them, through them, to them, and whatever is going on around them, to them and to others. This type of reflecting on one's whole 'being' in place and time, as understood by Groome, is to reflect on present praxis. Thus one's praxis is consciousness of one's whole 'being' in the world as agent-subject-in relationship.[17]

SCPA involves a focusing activity followed by five movements as follows:

FOCUSING ACT: 'The focusing activity turns people to their own "being" in place and time.'[18] Groome suggests that the focusing act is tied to interests, not just honouring the existing interests of participants, but also generating interests, as long as they actively engage people. Therefore, for instance, a facilitator might begin the first week as follows: 'Today we begin a five-week programme where we will explore what really is important to us. Perhaps it can be a special moment for us to attend to our own wells of hope, fear, joy, or anxiety. What brought you here this evening? What are your expectations as you approach this series of workshops? What hope, expectation, joy, or anxiety are you bringing to the group tonight?'

MOVEMENT 1: Groome describes the essential task of the first movement as offering 'an expression of present praxis of the theme, so that participants can perceive what is going on … regarding this issue in their lives'.[19] The programme invites initial expression from life around the theme by asking questions that evoke people's consciousness of their own present praxis. For instance, in the first week, the focusing act centres on a Robbie Williams song, 'Feel'. The ensuing questions include:

- What sense do you get from the song?
- What do you think the singer is looking for?
- Make a list of your own deepest needs in life. Do you hear any echo of what you are looking for?

Notice how the progression moves from what the singer is looking for (focusing act) to what participants identify as *their own* deepest needs and longings.

MOVEMENT 2: The aim here is to bring participants 'beyond recognition to some level of critical reflection' regarding present praxis.[20] Groome advises that reflection can draw from reason, memory and imagination. Here, questions are paramount; for instance, asking from where did you get that image; what does this text mean to you; what do you hear in the context of your own life? For instance, again in the first week, we move from the Robbie Williams song to the Webb Sisters singing Leonard Cohen's 'If It Be Your Will'. The questions that follow asks participants to compare the meaning inherent in the two pieces and then asks 'what does it mean to you?'

MOVEMENT 3: The aim of the previous movements is to enable people to come to recognise their own stories and visions of the learning experience that they now bring into dialogue with some aspect of the Christian Story/Vision. Movement 3 involves seeking the practical wisdom of the aspect, 'done with the practical intent for these people's lives'.[21] At this point, the programme invites participants to share some thoughts prompted by the content and to think about what sense it makes in their lives. The paradigm of education resonant here is that of Jesus with the Samaritan woman (John 4). As their conversation develops, the woman moves from seeing Jesus as enemy (Jew) to seeing him as prophet, and finally she recognises him as the Christ. In other words, the 'pedagogy' of Jesus allows the Samaritan woman to see for herself. The hope of Movement 3 is that participants will disclose the Christian Story Vision for themselves – *why* did they hear what they heard? In this movement, people are not expected to defend their positions; rather they are invited to go a little deeper and examine the hopes, expectations, images and stories they hold, which influence what is brought to mind and heart.

Staying with the first week, the aspect of the Christian Story/ Vision presented is divine revelation through Scripture, tradition and human experience. The questions that follow include:

- Name an experience when you have felt the presence of God
- How was that presence made 'known' (revealed) to you?
- How was God calling you to respond?

This is an example of Movement 3 at work.

MOVEMENT 4: At this point the programme provides space for people to stop, to look, to listen, and rather than simply co-relate the message, to integrate it. Again, this can be done by a series of reflective questions that ask, in one way or another, what are you coming to see for yourself; what wisdom does this passage have for your life? For instance, towards the end of the first week is a section entitled 'The Courage to Meet God'. This section asks: what relevance has all of this for you? In other words, does the Christian understanding of our longing for God, God's longing for us and God's constant revelation have any meaning for your life? Take some time to reflect. The following questions might help in the reflection process:

- Where do you see God in your work?
- What can help you recognise God in your everyday?

The ensuing discussion often involves very real reflections on how difficult it can be to educate in a particular way, on the obstacles to good teaching and learning in noisy, crowded classrooms, or on opportunities to develop a personal relationship with God.

MOVEMENT 5: A shared praxis style invites participants to make decisions around the generative theme and its practical implications. This movement is really about making decisions for one's own life in light of the previous four movements. Groome's advice is to pose questions that invite participants' own praxis-like decisions and responses, such as: what are you thinking; what does this mean for how you live your life? What does this mean for your work as an educator; for your students; for how you teach and, ultimately, why you teach? It is here that the pedagogy challenges us to look beyond the content of our teaching, which often seems to be our primary concern, to take equal care of who we are teaching, where this takes place, and how we go about it.

For instance, the closing questions of Week 1 include:

- If you chose to build a relationship with God, how would you go about doing that?
- What have you learned today that might be helpful for your own life?

From my experience of SCPA, Movement 5 is most likely to take place in a prayerful environment. This is one reason why every week allows time and space for a closing prayer – although the form this takes differs from week to week.

The Five Movements in summary
The focusing act and five movements follow Groome's dynamic of bringing *life to Faith to life*. Let me set out a bird's-eye view of them with a description of the curricular intent of each movement, within a community of conversation.

Focusing Act: Establishing the curriculum around a life or faith generative theme.

	MOVEMENT 1 (M1):	Expressing the theme in present praxis.
LIFE		
	MOVEMENT 2 (M2):	Reflecting critically on the theme
to		
FAITH	MOVEMENT 3 (M3):	Presenting Christian Story/Vision with meaning and persuasion
to		
	MOVEMENT 4 (M4):	Appropriating the truths and wisdom of Christian faith into life
LIFE		
	MOVEMENT 5 (M5):	Making decisions in light of Christian faith

Groome's shared praxis approach invites people to come to a lived faith. For this to work, we need to reach people's lives, hearts, what matters to them. Groome sees this approach as a type of presence, a way of being with people. He draws our attention to the importance of crafting good questions – questions that are not merely intellectual, but appeal also to the affective, that draw from

111

the lived experience of the participants, whoever they might be. He stresses the importance of open questions that bring them into, yet somehow out of, their own worlds.

SCPA at work

Groome's SCPA brings home the importance of good preparation, of personal style (which he advises us to hold lightly), and of intentionality. For instance, the focus on good conversation must emanate not from coercion but from invitation. If we want to create a listening environment that is also a sharing environment, we need to listen well, to avoid technological language, to aim towards a trusting environment where every person is comfortable not only to share, but to hear the contributions of others. The overarching commitment is to create a community of participation and conversation to integrate life and faith. For this, the particular commitments include engagement, expression, reflection, access, appropriation and decision.

The ultimate aim of *Joining the Dots* is personal appropriation of at least some aspects of Christian faith that help us to live well. But spirituality assumes an active faith and this is the gift of Groome's SCPA – the understanding that real education is ultimately about bringing life to faith and back to life. The increasing transfer of religious beliefs from the public realm to the private individual makes it hard for people, even colleagues, to discuss issues of religion and spirituality in a public forum. Yet this is precisely what *Joining the Dots* attempts to do. By building on the already existing bonds of collegiality and community in a familiar and comfortable setting, the programme with its Shared Praxis Approach encourages people to engage with the content, make sense of it for themselves and share their wisdom with colleagues.

The context of catechetical education

'The Christian community is the origin, locus, and goal of catechesis,'[22] and that faith community includes 'the family, parish, Catholic schools, Christian associations and movements, basic ecclesial communities'.[23] Whereas it began as a school-based programme, *Joining the Dots* can be used in and by any of these groups. The text is such that little adaptation of the content is needed.

The pedagogy remains the same. The only adaptation a particular facilitator may need is to align it with their own style, or with the interests of a particular group.

The content of catechetical education

The *GDC* makes clear that the 'content' of catechesis is 'the Gospel message' as represented by a comprehensive presentation of Catholic Christian faith. Here 'Sacred Scripture should have a pre-eminent position'[24] as given 'an authentic interpretation by the Church's magisterium'.[25] The *Catechism of the Catholic Church* (*CCC*) is 'the doctrinal point of reference for all catechesis'.[26]

The *GDC* insists that this content not be presented as a purely cognitive exercise. Christian faith has 'cognitive, experiential, and behavioural'[27] aspects. It goes on to say that this holistic sense of faith is reflected in the ancient language of *lex credendi, lex orandi* and *lex vivendi* – pertaining to what Christians are to *believe*, how they are to *pray* and worship, and how they are to *live* their faith in the world.[28]

In short, the *GDC* calls for catechetical education that includes all the essential aspects of Catholic Christian faith and that presents this faith as a holistic affair, engaging people's heads, hearts and hands. The programme follows this approach. The definitive aim is to put people in communion, in intimacy, with Jesus Christ and the triune God. It therefore hopes for a Christological centrality to form the content of instruction, to be a vehicle for growth in relationship, to know him and live according to the truth he has given to us. At the same time, all religious education should reflect good scholarship and the invitation is offered for people to think for themselves in order to appropriate the faith as their own. 'The faithful ... should be accorded a lawful freedom of inquiry, of thought, and of expression.'[29] This is clearly the content of *Joining the Dots*, laid out in specific terms in Chapter 5, The Theology and Spirituality of *Joining the Dots*.

Other pedagogical aspects

Spirituality – defined concisely as faith at work – is the undercurrent of the programme, reflected in two particular ways. First, the teaching dynamic attempts to engage the 'souls' of participants, from beginning to end of each lesson – what they really think and feel, what they come to make their own, how they decide to live their faith. Second, in presenting the 'content' of Christian Faith, there is attention to its spiritual wisdom, emphasising how this is a life-giving way to live in the world. Each week begins with a 'great question' of pressing relevance to educators – some real issue for their lives posed as an engaging and generative theme. This theme is then brought to the resources of Catholic Faith for its spiritual wisdom – especially as incarnate in Jesus Christ – in order to bring it back to life again as owned spiritual wisdom, as lived Christian Faith in the world. Each week concludes with a closing prayer, using different prayer forms.

Joining the Dots takes seriously the intense encounter of all age groups today with digital media and technology. The suggested reading at the conclusion of each week includes relevant websites, and the programme suggests a 'praying with digital media' experience (from www.loyolapress.com) in Week 5. However, as digital media and technology have become so dominant in the everyday, *Joining the Dots* deliberately tries to be as gadget-free as possible in order to establish an 'old-fashioned' prayer environment, so to speak. As Charles Dickens once remarked, 'electric communication will never be a substitute for the face of someone who with their soul encourages another person to be brave and true'.[30] This of course is at the discretion of the facilitator; in a noisy, busy, electronic world, I have found that it provides a welcome contrast.

The programme content strongly emphasises that Christian faith is 'good news', that it represents great hope for people today and the potential of finding true happiness in life. However, it also emphasises that living as a Christian presents a real challenge, that being a disciple of Jesus brings personal and social responsibilities. The balance of both consolation and challenge, of hope and demand, go hand in hand.

In keeping with contemporary literature on teaching, the pedagogy reflects a commitment to collaborative learning, frequently encouraging participants to work as partners. The dynamic of structured conversation is crucial here.[31] Education is sacred territory dealing with the very heart of the person. The idea is not so much to facilitate God's 'breaking into' a profane world at certain points, as to help people to experience the 'breaking out' of God's own self, already and always present at the heart of the world. In opening up conversation by asking good questions, facilitators must be certain to avoid answering those questions themselves. The pedagogy depends on participants bringing their own experiences into dialogue with the Christian Story/Vision. SCPA stands or falls on the ability of the facilitator to manage time well, listen carefully, ask good questions, ensure a balance of all voices are respectfully heard and avoid the temptation to fill the silences. The wisdom of the group – regardless of the profile of the participants – is paramount.

NOTES

1. Daniel J. O'Leary, *Begin with the Heart, the Harvest Will Follow: Recovering a Sacramental Vision for Pastoral Ministry and Personal Wholeness* (Dublin: Columba Press, 2008).

2. Congregation for the Clergy, *General Directory for Catechesis* (Washington DC: United States Catholic Conference, 1997).

3. Ibid.

4. *The General Directory of Catechesis* (*GDC*) is the most recent comprehensive statement on catechesis from the magisterium and as such represents the official mind of the Catholic Church on these matters.

5. *Gaudium et Spes*, n. 43, in Austin Flannery OP (ed.), *Vatican Council II: The Basic Sixteen Documents* (Dublin: Dominican Publications, 1996).

6. Philip F. Lawler, 'Pew Survey Shows America's Vast Catholic Exodus', www.catholicculture.org/news/features/index.cfm?recnum=56894 (accessed 6 December 2011).

7. Cited in *Begin with the Heart*, 71.

8. *GDC*, nn. 205–207.

9. Ibid.

10. I outline what I mean by critical correlation as a theological method in Chapter 3.

11. Thomas H. Groome, *Sharing Faith: A Comprehensive Approach to Religious Education and Pastoral Ministry* (Eugene, Oregon: Wipf & Stock, 1991).

12. For an in-depth examination of SCPA, read ibid. A more accessible account is given in Thomas H. Groome, *Will There Be Faith? Depends on Every Christian* (Dublin: Veritas, 2011).

13. Thomas H. Groome, *Educating for Life: A Spiritual Vision for Every Teacher and Parent* (Allen, Texas: T. More, 1998); *Will There Be Faith: Depends on Every Christian*.

14. Groome, *Sharing Faith*, 430.

15. Groome uses the term 'Christian Story/Vision' to remind us that every time we relate some aspect of the Christian story, we also need to raise up the vision, so that rather than merely learning *about* the content, we learn *from* it, and see for ourselves the implications for good education and healthy spirituality. The Story stretches back through Scripture and Tradition, from which we can draw great wisdom for the present; Vision looks into the future, presenting us with ways and challenges to live and work towards the Kingdom. The Christian vision is 'for life for all'; God's will done on earth as it is in heaven.

16. Groome, *Will There Be Faith?*, 275–80.

17. For more detail on this, see Groome, *Sharing Faith*.

18. Ibid., 146.

19. Ibid., 376.

20. Ibid.

21. Ibid.

22. *GDC*, n. 245.

23. Ibid., n. 253.

24. Ibid., n. 127.

25. Ibid., nn. 95, 96.

26. Ibid., nn. 93, 121.

27. Ibid., n. 35.

28. Ibid., n. 122.

29. Flannery (ed.), *Vatican Council II: The Basic Sixteen Documents*; *GS*, n. 62.

30. This is an adaptation of text in a collaborative work by Dickens entitled 'The Wreck of the Golden Mary'. http://www.brainyquote.com/quotes/keywords/soul_7.html#ixzz1dmd2Z6Oo (accessed 6 December 2011).

31. See Chapter 2: Facilitating *Joining the Dots*.

five
The Theology and Spirituality of *Joining the Dots*

For this soul needs to be honoured with a new dress woven
From green and blue things and arguments that cannot be
proven.
(Patrick Kavanagh, 'Canal Bank Walk')[1]

Theological Method and *Joining the Dots*
Christianity has always had to articulate what it means to live in the world as a disciple of Jesus Christ. This has manifested itself in different ways over the centuries. In his classic work *Christ and Culture*, H. Richard Niebuhr outlined five approaches – Christ against culture, Christ of culture, Christ above culture, Christ and culture in paradox, and Christ the transformer of culture.[2] *Joining the Dots* places its emphasis on the contribution of Christianity to the transformation of culture and the person. It does this through the use of conversation, or in more theological terms, through the use of 'revised critical correlation'. Let me say a word about theological correlation and then about revised theological correlation.

Theological correlation 'emphasises the importance of theology's engagement with contemporary culture'.[3] This engagement can take different forms in various contexts at given times. For instance, St Paul engaged with the Athenians in a particular way when he stood in front of the council of the Areopagus:

> Men of Athens, I have seen for myself how extremely scrupulous you are in all religious matters, because I noticed, as I strolled round admiring your sacred monuments, that you had an altar inscribed: 'To An Unknown God.' Well, the God whom I proclaim is in fact the one whom you already worship without knowing it. (Acts 17:23)

Paul spoke to them in a way that made use of their own images and values. He entered their world and affirmed their search for truth and for God. *Joining the Dots* seeks to do likewise. It brings the Christian tradition into conversation with the life experience of the participants; it attempts to make the wisdom of that tradition accessible and intelligible to people who work in Catholic settings.

Paul's ability to connect with the questions of others, to use their language and idiom to communicate Christian faith is central to correlational theology. The concern that theology must engage with the existential and moral questions of each generation is ongoing. In the middle of the last century, Paul Tillich sought a way for theology to offer a source of understanding that makes it possible to live meaningfully. He proposed that theologians need to pay close attention to the culture, to listen to the questions being asked and to offer a response that is both theologically authentic and understandable to that culture.

> The answers implied in the event of revelation are meaningful
> only in so far as they are in correlation with questions
> concerning the whole of our existence ... Only those who
> have experienced the shock of transitoriness, the anxiety in
> which they are aware of their finitude, the threat of non-being,
> can understand what the notion of God means. Only those
> who have experienced the tragic ambiguities of our historical
> existence and have totally questioned the meaning of existence
> can understand what the symbol of God means ...[4]

Tillich sought to make Christianity understandable and relevant to people in the context of their own lives and questions. However, his correlation presumed a non-critical exchange between the gospel and culture, more of an application than a dialectical correlation.

David Tracy sought to correct this and built on the work of Tillich. For Tracy, theology ought to be at the interface of human experience and Christian truth claims. Theology is not just a resource for the questions of the day, a place where answers are to be found – it is also a partner in the conversation, and as such is open to new insights about its own identity and beliefs. Theology has learned from the lived experience of people. For instance, over the centuries it has learned that slavery is wrong and shifted its stance on the importance of democracy; it has come to promote human rights throughout the world and appreciate the urgent need to care for the environment.

Conversation and Theology

The metaphor of conversation is helpful in understanding the dynamic that takes place when human experience and the Christian tradition are brought into contact with one another. There is a dialectical dimension to the heart of any good conversation. It is characterised by a back-and-forth movement between partners, an exchange between the 'gospel' and the culture, the culture and the 'gospel'. Within this conversation, there are three possible moments: 'one of affirming, giving assent, or accepting; a moment of questioning and possibly of refusing or negating';[5] and a moment 'of moving one to new and transformed possibilities for both "gospel" and culture'.[6] In such a conversation, Christian belief might affirm dimensions of the culture as being congruent with its own deepest convictions; or there may be parts of the culture that Christian faith queries or rejects as being opposed to God's reign. However, conversation moves in both directions. Consequently, where faith and life are brought into conversation, there may be aspects of Christian faith that are called into question by the conversation partners.

The poet David Whyte says that conversation is something from which we should not emerge intact. It ought to enlarge our understanding of ourselves, others and creation. David Tracy defines conversation this way:

> Conversation is a game with some hard rules: say only what you mean; say it as accurately as you can; listen to and respect what the other says, however different or other; be willing to correct or defend your opinions if challenged by the conversation partner; be willing to argue if necessary, to confront if demanded, to endure necessary conflict, to change your mind if the evidence suggests it.[7]

Conversation and interpretation

Conversation is complex and requires real participation, far more than takes place in a chat or a casual encounter with another. When entered into as Tracy suggests, it can be transformative. However, we must realise that when we enter into conversation with others, we are all the time engaged in interpretation. All our perceptions of others are based on interpretation. We project meaning onto them, and these projected meanings, our prejudices (or our pre-judging), need to be checked out to see if they are valid, or distortions, or a bit of both. It is not possible to check them out on our own; only when our interpretations are provoked do we notice them in the first place.[8] Only when we are 'pulled up short', only when there is a dissonance between what we believe and some new perspective, do we begin to intuit the need for further reflection. New understanding will happen at the in-between of what is familiar and what is strange. The art of good questioning can bring us there. Questions open up possibilities and engage assumptions. Allowing ourselves to ask questions or be asked questions is risky; older understandings and ways of seeing the world might be found wanting and require adjustment. This movement, this back and forth, is at the very heart of the theology of *Joining the Dots*.

When we are in conversation with someone or with a text[9] for the first time, we find ourselves agreeing, disagreeing, surprised or confused in varying combinations and degrees of intensity. These are our initial interpretative reactions, our first impressions. To listen better and understand more fully the position of another, we must temporarily suspend concern for our own position on a particular issue. This will help us grasp the point that the other is making. Not to be equated with a facile agreement with the other's position, this is an attempt to 'build a bridge of trust and mutual respect for the subsequent negotiation of differences in interest and perspective'.[10] It is only when we have come to understand the position and interest of another that the back-and-forth movement of authentic conversation may begin to unfold in a transformative manner. The challenging, confirming, negating, confusing, surprising, reassuring, disturbing, comforting dynamics of the conversation can jolt us and help reveal our presuppositions and enlarge our understanding of the issue at hand. This is part of the reason group work is important.

Participants are helped to come to know what they believe and value through the questioning and promptings of others. In recognising what they believe, they can then evaluate its trustworthiness for their lives today. Over the weeks of the programme, trust grows among participants and makes sustained, critical conversation possible.

When a conversation gets to this level, the participants must be prepared to 'submit all positions to a critical and creative suspicion, to expose and challenge systematic biases on both sides.'[11] This process can involve people in the four transcendental precepts proposed by Bernard Lonergan: conversation helps us tend to our experience of the data, to understand the intelligible, to judge the truth, and to be responsible for the good.[12] The bringing together of theology and experience, or faith and life, in a conversational manner is essential if faith is not to be marginalised and shrunk to fit the private dimension of our lives together. This is the aim of *Joining the Dots*.

Spirituality and *Joining the Dots*

The human search for God is as old as humanity itself. It is an ongoing, ardent enterprise, common to every culture and tradition no matter how advanced or primitive. Symbols and language may change over time, but the search goes on. It is a necessary phenomenon of human existence. Finding a critical correlation between faith and life can be a struggle. Not everyone working in Catholic schools is a committed Catholic; indeed there are those from other faith traditions and world views on their staffs. And as faith is not something static, once found kept unchanged, even those persons of committed faith will have moments of doubt, periods of wondering and adjustment.

Pope Benedict XVI suggests that the 'world of reason and the world of religious faith – the world of secular rationality and the world of religious belief – need one another and should not be afraid to enter into a profound and ongoing dialogue, for the good of our civilisation'.[13] Accepting the relationship between faith and reason, that deep faith and deep questioning go hand in hand, this programme seeks to open a dialogue with all those who are interested in questions of faith – those who are committed, those who are alienated, those who are indifferent, and those who are coming to consider questions of faith for the first time.

At the same time, evangelisation is and always has been the heart of the Christian mission. The task of the Christian community is to proclaim in words and deeds the Good News revealed in Jesus Christ, through the Spirit, that we are loved by God for all eternity, for God is love (1 Jn 4:8, 16). The teachings of Jesus Christ and the challenges he presents make sense only in this light.

A five-week programme is a limited venture. Even so, it must attempt to present an overview of the Christian Story/Vision.[14] The operative image, rather than a hierarchy of truths, is more the Celtic spiral. The Christian tradition suggests two central mysteries – two concepts which lie at the spiral core – Trinity and Incarnation. Then, in the Catholic expression of the Christian tradition, we honour the sacramental principle. It follows then that the questions at the heart of the programme include: who or what is God/what are the dominant images of God from our Judeo-Christian tradition; what does Jesus tell us about God and about ourselves; how does the Spirit of God live today and how does it relate to the human spirit/where and how do we see and relate to this triune God in everyday life? These central questions form the interlacing themes of the five weeks.

Defining 'Spirituality'

I see spirituality as central to every educator (indeed, every person), no matter who they are, where they work, or who or what they teach. It does not assume any particular religious tradition or religious faith at all, although when in positive, dynamic relationship, spirituality and religion can be mutually enriching. But it does account for the search for what is meaningful in life, and places this search within a transcendent horizon. Parker Palmer's description of spirituality as the heart's longing to be connected with the largeness of life resonates here.[15] However, there is another dimension to spirituality. Nicholas Lash has remarked, 'My mistrust of contemporary interest in "spirituality" arises from the suspicion that quite a lot of material set out in book stores under this description sells because it does not stretch the mind or challenge our behaviour. It tends to soothe rather than subvert our well-heeled complacency.'[16] Lash's comments imply that spirituality must do more than keep people within their comfort zones; it needs to push them beyond themselves towards something other than themselves.

The work of Sandra Schneiders is particularly useful in coining a working definition of spirituality appropriate to the programme. According to Schneiders, although spirituality can be both stranger and rival to religion, healthy spirituality can also be a partner with religious traditions. Spirituality and religious traditions can be partners in mutually beneficial ways. Spirituality that lacks the structural and functional resources of religious tradition is rootless and often fruitless for both the person and society; religion that is uninformed by a lived spirituality is dead and often deadly. It can become purely ideological or wither to rigid routine.

Schneiders proposes that spirituality has two distinguishing features. First, it is an *anthropological constant*. By this she means that, like personality, spirituality is a characteristic of the human person, whether one recognises it or not. Although all humans are spiritual in this basic anthropological sense, each person develops his or her spirituality in a unique and personal way (just as every person develops a unique personality). Every human person has a capacity for spirituality. However, spirituality as a developed relationality (rather than a capacity) is not universal. In other words, while everyone has the innate capacity to live a spiritual life, not everyone recognises and nurtures this capacity.

Second, for Schneiders, spirituality is a *life project or practice* involving life-integration and self-transcendence toward ultimate value. It is the capacity of persons to transcend themselves, to reach beyond themselves in relationship to others; acting on this capacity is a conscious, life-long enterprise, which brings the person beyond themselves towards what they perceive to be of ultimate value. Schneiders is quick to point out that ultimate value is objective rather than merely subjective. Thus one might perceive life itself, the health of the earth, justice for all people, or union with God as ultimate value. In summary, Schneiders defines spirituality as 'the experience of conscious involvement in the project of life integration through self-transcendence toward the ultimate value one perceives'.[17]

Spirituality and religious tradition
Spirituality is always contextual; it takes on a different form depending on the context within which it operates. Spirituality

is often but not always contextualised by religion. For instance, spirituality in a Catholic school is embodied in the Catholic Christian tradition.

When we apply Schneiders' general definition of spirituality to the specific tradition of Christianity, we encounter a religious spirituality where the ultimate value is the triune God revealed in Jesus Christ, in whose life we share through the gift of the Spirit in the context of the Christian community. The desired life-integration is personal transformation in Christ, which implies participation in the transformation of the world in justice for all creatures. Thus any attempt to foster Christian spirituality must have as its centre the personal lived relationship with Jesus Christ. The community is the locus for this spirituality, for it is in the community, the body of Christ, that one is to encounter the One who is Love (1 Jn 4:16).

Ignatian spirituality and *Joining the Dots*

The spiritual emphasis in *Joining the Dots* is primarily Christocentric. However, the gospels contain many emphases of Jesus – his time in the wilderness, his healing, his poverty and passion. They have all led to various kinds of spirituality and give rise to the distinctive features we find with, for example, Dominican, Franciscan and Benedictine spiritualities, to name but a few. *Joining the Dots* is rooted in Ignatian spirituality as one particularly appropriate to the world of education and educators. Grounded in Christian theology, it holds key features common to every integrative Christian spirituality; it is simply the nuance or emphasis that changes. The nature of the Ignatian charism is suited to teaching, as born out by the success of Jesuit education over a 500-year history. The substantive pedagogy and school system to which it gave rise is clearly rooted in Ignatian spirituality.

Hallmarks of Ignatian spirituality

Ignatian spirituality fits into the larger reality of human spiritual hunger. Today's 'transcendent spirituality', according to Robert J. Starratt, is characterised by 'a whole new consciousness of personal and social identity, a new sense of community' and a new social, political and ethical response to the ecological crisis.[18] It resonates deeply with the native creation spiritualities and their awareness of God's presence in everything. At the same time, its solidarity with global crises moves beyond empathy and demands a human response. This juxtaposition of belonging and response is also the hallmark (known as the Principle and Foundation – the vocation of every person to love and service) of Ignatian spirituality. Framed in this context, and with its triadic dynamic between self, God and responding in words and deeds to what is other, especially to whom and what is in need of help, it is clear that Ignatian spirituality has much to offer in the contemporary climate.

Every spirituality develops in response to the movements of a particular time, culture and set of circumstances. The story of Ignatius of Loyola, his dramatic conversion and the cultural context of his era has been told many times. It is not my intention to repeat it here. What is significant to this project is the story of his evolving spirituality. Ignatius was virtually illiterate in matters theological and spiritual when he began his spiritual journey.[19] During his recovery after the fall of Pamplona, he realised that God could stir his heart to draw him in one direction, but that there was an enemy of God who was trying to draw his heart in a different and conflicting direction. Because he could not identify any reason why God would single him out, he became convinced that God was calling everyone to intimacy and service – a remarkably optimistic expectation and high anthropology. This constitutes the foundational reality, the Principle and Foundation, of Ignatian spirituality.

Finding God in all things constituted Ignatius' own inner attitude: 'He found God not only in quiet prayer; but also in the confused messiness of his daily work, with all of its problems and concerns, as well as in his ordinary conversations with others.'[20] Ignatius realised that God works through the ordinary events of every day; the challenge to humanity is to find God in all things, events, and circumstances of daily living,[21] and to respond with loving service.

There is little that is new in such a positive cosmology. Ignatius' contribution was the praxis emphasis: the inclusion of attention to images, desires and feelings as sources of God's self-disclosure to the person, and the tracking of personal behaviour and attitudes which effectively reveal or blind us to God's presence and invitation in the bits and pieces of everyday life.

Ignatius developed rules for discerning the spirits and for testing what is of God and what is not. Discernment of spirits is another hallmark of Ignatian spirituality and is directed toward interpreting one's life and the decisions to be made. Eventually he developed what he called the examen in order to recognise the movements of God's Spirit in ordinary experience. The examen, meant to be undertaken by a person twice a day, is simply a quiet moment of taking stock. Born out of a sense of gratitude for the gracious goodness of God, the person reflects on the events of the day and looks for patterns of the Spirit's movements over time. Like all Ignatian spiritual practices, it is conducted without self-praise or blame; the idea is to track how we allow God's presence into our lives and how we block or turn away from that presence through our human sinfulness.

His Basque biographer Tellechea Idígoras insists that, like John of the Cross or Teresa of Avila, Ignatius was a very great mystic, although the wrapping is different. 'Before anything else, he was a man infused with the gifts of the Holy Spirit, one who listened to God all of the time.'[22] In Ignatius' case however, mysticism is not withdrawal from normal activities or the isolated life. It is an awareness of God's presence in all things, which is then responded to as loving service.

Some theological features of Ignatian spirituality (as they apply to the programme)

1. Trinity

The Triune God of Christian tradition is more a reality of experience than a question to be pondered. If Trinity is a central mystery of Christian faith, then it should affect everything – how we relate to God, to others, to ourselves. It should shape our spirituality and our prayer lives. Trinity is central not only for understanding who God is but what we're invited into. Far from being disconnected from everyday spirituality, the Trinity names the activities of God that reflect God's very selfhood. To say it is a mystery should not mean that it is remote or has no relevance for our everyday lives.

The history of spiritual direction tells us that we have known God in all God's ways (i.e. three sets of operations) without putting them together in a complete, comprehensive whole. At different times we relate to God as:

- Father/Mother/Creator/Source/Origin
- Christ/Liberator/Redeemer/Healer
- Spirit/Sustainer/Sanctifier/Guide.

At any moment in time we are likely to be relating to God in one way more dominantly than the other two. When we are comfortable with three persons in one, then, when the flux of life demands, we can pray primarily to one of those over another; one more than another may become the focus of prayer. I remember when I discovered I was pregnant with my first baby feeling an overwhelming surge toward the Spirit. The line from the Nicene Creed kept flooding into my mind: 'We believe in the Holy Spirit ... the Giver of Life.' The giver of life that was still, through me, giving new life. And although one might think that God the Father-Creator would become the centre of my prayer, it was in fact a whole new sense of the Spirit, the life-giving, ongoing Spirit that took over.

Our religious experience doesn't really tell of all these three dimensions at once. Yet generations of Christians have experienced God in these patterns. Who God is within Godself and who God is in relation to us is inextricably bound – God's inner life and our participation in that life. We have come to realise that these three persons or energies are distinct, but the unity of God rests in mutual interdependence of these three persons. Of course, if we are made in the image and likeness of God, then we also are made to be interdependent, in radical relation. This is quite different to a society that favours the autonomous person whose goal is independence and self-fulfilment. Contemporary theologians such as David Tracy want us to re-grasp that who God is in relation to Godself mirrors exactly who God is in relation to us. According to Tracy, radical relationality is God's primary attribute and therefore what we are called to become. The perfection of God lies in this radical relationality – in terms of interconnections. This is very different to how we have construed perfection. Once we understand that, we can grasp that we are being invited into union with God through union with each other. Of course this is what Jesus tries to teach with the Golden Rule.

The invitation of the Trinity

According to Michael Downey, the Trinity means that 'God's face is immutably turned toward us in love, that God's presence to us is utterly reliable and constant.'[23] This presence is a force, a movement, a life pulsing toward us in love. The doctrine of the Trinity tries to put words on this mystery of God. It conceives of God as a 'dynamism of divine love' and points out that

> God's very being, what it is for God *to be*, is loving, life-giving relationality. God does not just *have* a love relationship with us, God is loving relationality. There is no self-contained, divine individual residing in heaven far away from us; there is simply a dynamic movement of divine love, which *is* God.[24]

Being created in the image and likeness of this Triune God, this loving relationality – called to live as people of God – means that we too need to be in relationships that are characterised by self-gift, mutuality and interdependence. Our imaging of God grounds the ethical demands of the Christian life. We are invited to be in communion with the world around us, to be in right relationship with others, especially those who are excluded and poor, with our very selves and with the whole cosmos – and in this way, in right relationship with God.

This demand is echoed in Jesus' own preaching of the two great commandments. In the Synoptic Gospels (Mt 22:34-40; Mk 12:28-31; Lk 10:25-28), Jesus was asked about the greatest commandment of the Mosaic code. At that time, there were two answers to this question. One was that the greatest commandment was to love God with all one's heart, soul and strength, the other to love your neighbour as yourself. In the view of the day, these were two separate commandments.[25] However, in the answer Jesus gave to the question, he fused them together, saying they were one and the same. According to Michael Himes, 'It is not a case of loving God and loving our neighbour; loving God is loving our neighbour; loving our neighbour is loving God. They are identical.'[26] That is because 'God is love' (1 Jn 4:8, 16). God is 'what happens between and among us, is the foundation of the possibility of our loving one another at all.'[27] We are *in* God, in a loving relationship, one that makes it possible for us to love one another and at the same time to discover the presence of God in the in-between of our relationships.

In a Trinitarian spirituality, God does not compete for the love I have for my husband, family or friends. In loving them, I am participating in the love of God. God is what holds us in relationship and moves between those in the relationship; the love 'in-between'. Further, a Trinitarian spirituality cares about the whole of life. It is not one dimension among others in a life of faith. It is concerned with our own integration and the ability of all to flourish in this life; living in accord with the power and presence of the Holy Spirit, who conforms us to Jesus Christ.

Trinity and *Joining the Dots*

Having unpacked this mystery somewhat, the pastoral implications become clear. Most significantly, Trinity can influence (a) our ways of entry into prayer, and (b) our ways of perceiving God and what we are invited into. As a central mystery, Trinity provides the framework for *Joining the Dots*.

There is a Trinitarian circularity to the programme. The entire universe proceeds from God and returns to God; the end of the programme corresponds to the beginning. The God of the opening sequence who reaches out to Adam in Michelangelo's classic depiction is the same God in the closing moments who desires union with every educator and their community. The Spirit that breathes through the programme teaching us to pray is of course the Holy Spirit of the Christian tradition. So too is the indwelling of God's ongoing presence in ourselves and in all things. The Jesus of history whose virtue, values and ethic we lift up in Week 2 is the same Christ of Faith of Week 4, present in our education communities. God as Father and Creator in Week 3 points to God as transcendent; the presence of God in all things in all events of our daily lives points to the immanent God whose presence is experienced within (Week 5). Weeks 1 to 3 proceed from God the Spirit through God the Son to God the Father; Weeks 3 to 5 proceed in reverse circularity – from God the Father through God the Son to God the Spirit. Thus Weeks 1 and 5 are pneumatological in emphasis, Weeks 2 and 4 Christological, with God the Father as the centrepiece in Week 3.

2. Incarnation

A specific Christian understanding of God can never be separated from the revelation of God in Jesus Christ. For Christians, being human is essentially linked to one's relationship to Jesus Christ. But who is Jesus Christ? There are many answers to this question: teacher, historical figure, the Messiah, half God, half man, a moral example, the face of God, radical Palestinian Jew. However one answers this question, most Christians at least admire him. But, theologians ask, is admiration enough? We can admire people from a distance, without their lives making any claim on ours. For instance, we can admire Aung San Suu Kyi and be unmoved by the struggle for justice of the Burmese; we can admire Mother Teresa without caring for the poor. Jesus wants more than our admiration, even more than imitation. Rather, Jesus wants us to experience his presence, to respond to his invitation of friendship. As John Shea puts it, Jesus is not a law to be obeyed or a model to be imitated, but a presence to be seized and acted upon.[28] He expresses this sentiment beautifully in his poem below:

Sharon's Christmas Prayer[29]

She was five,
sure of the facts,
and recited them
with slow solemnity
convinced every word was revelation.
She said
They were so poor
They had only peanut butter and jelly sandwiches to eat
and they went a long way from home
without getting lost. The lady rode
a donkey, the man walked, and the baby
was inside the lady.
They had to stay in a stable
with an ox and an ass (hee-hee)
but the Three Rich Men found them
because a star lited the roof
Shepherds came and you could
pet the sheep but not feed them.

Then the baby was borned.
And do you know who he was?
Her quarter eyes inflated to silver dollars.
The baby was God.
And she jumped in the air
whirled round, dove into the sofa
and buried her head under the cushion
which is the only proper response
to the Good News of the Incarnation.

Elizabeth Johnson reminds us that something incomparably good happens to people in their encounter with Jesus Christ. They come to themselves, being resorted to inner integrity. Relationships with self and others are healed and peace becomes a real possibility. Given the profound impact of Jesus Christ in their lives, the question inevitably arises – who is he? This is a question the programme asks, challenging participants to decide for themselves – who is Jesus for them in their lives right now?

In Jesus, two natures, human and divine, have come together. Jesus was both fully human and fully divine at the same time. Since Jesus was the closest human person to God, his divinity – his intimate connection with God – allowed him to be the most human person that has ever lived. The other side of the coin is that closeness to God makes us more human. Humanity and divinity are not opposites. The closer we are to God, the more fully human and free we become. Jesus' divinity allowed him to be fully human, truly himself and radically free. If we want to know what it really means to be human, then we need to look at the life of Jesus to see what it means to be fully alive.

A central mystery of Christianity is the Incarnation but our familiarity with the story can hinder our capacity to appreciate its immensity. Many think of the Incarnation as an historical event – the result of God's love and care for humanity. God sent Jesus into the world two thousand years ago. He was truly God and truly human. He had two natures. He was the face of God to the world. He lived with integrity, doing his Father's will. He healed the sick, reached out to the poor, included women in his ministry, challenged the authorities of the day, and he performed miracles. Then, those who plotted against him, from the beginning of his public ministry, had him put to death on a cross. He rose again from the dead, brought his followers to a hillside outside and ascended physically to heaven – the Incarnation. But that is only half the story or perhaps only the beginning. While it is true to believe that the physical body of Jesus was with us for thirty-three years, it is not true to think that that was the end of the Incarnation. The Incarnation is not only a past event. It is still ongoing today.

The ongoing Incarnation

While Jesus left the earth almost two thousand years ago, the body of Christ did not. Rather than a surname for Jesus, 'Christ' is a title referring to God's anointed one present in the world today. When we use the term 'Jesus Christ', we are referring to two realities: the human Jesus of history and the Christ of faith, the post-resurrection presence of Jesus. This presence is often referred to as the body of Christ. It signifies three things: Jesus, the historical Palestinian Jew, the Eucharist and the community of believers. It is important to realise that the Eucharist and the community of believers are not just the body of Christ in some analogical or metaphorical way. Rather, in both of these symbols, God is really, physically present. We Christians are the body of Christ in the world today. Teresa of Avila puts it this way:

Christ has no body now on earth but yours,
no hands but yours,
no feet but yours.
Yours are the eyes through which Christ's compassion must look out on the world.
Yours are the feet with which he is to go about doing good.
Yours are the hands with which he is to bless us now.

(St Teresa of Avila, 1515–82)

A key feature of the humanity of Jesus was his care and love for people on the margins of society. This has serious implications for how we are the Body of Christ in the world today. Jesus recognised the dignity in people who were poor, sick and sinful, a dignity that was eroded because of the culture of the day. He was able to see people as they are and not as society so ungenerously imagined them to be. His actions revealed the love that God has for the weak, vulnerable and silenced. The relationship that Jesus had with those who were poor in his own day challenges us in our relationship with those who are forgotten, invisible and excluded today.

Centredness on Christ with an education mission

I have already outlined how the spirituality of Ignatius of Loyola is one particularly suited to educators. Another reason for its suitability is its focus on Christ as a man on the move, negotiating the teachable moments as they so often arise. It is noticeable that relatively few of the Gospel stories assigned for prayerful reading in the Spiritual Exercises deal with miracles compared with those where Jesus is teaching and talking with people. Ignatius' Jesus is primarily a teacher who engages in a very real way with the needs of the time.

The Spiritual Exercises reveal a God who teaches the spiritual seeker directly. And so Ignatius himself became a teacher (through the Spiritual Exercises) and education became the foundation ministry of his society. *Joining the Dots* makes room for a God who directly teaches – through the use of a variety of Ignatian prayer forms, through quiet reflective time and space where participants can listen to the voice of God speaking in their own hearts, and through the Shared Christian Praxis Approach,[30] which encourages each person to appropriate and decide for themselves the meaning they derive from each week.

Behind Ignatius' medieval metaphors of crusading armies and kings lies what Paul's epistles describe as divine mystery. This mystery is that in Christ the world is reconciled to God (2 Cor 5:19). Christ's mission is to unite all things in himself and thereby to God (1 Th 5:9; Col 2:2; Eph 1:9-10). Every Christian is called to carry on this mission – to do his or her part in the divine project. Of course the point of the Spiritual Exercises is for the person making them to discern, at various points in life, how best they can play their part in bringing about the Kingdom. Although this theme runs through the programme, it is highlighted in a particular way in the final week. Thus the programme is Christocentric, referring both to the Jesus of history and the Christ of faith (Weeks 2 and 4 in particular), and centred on Jesus Christ with an education mission.

3. Sacramental Imagination

Deep familiarity with the revealed stories of creation (Week 3) and Incarnation allows all kinds of things to be seen as compelling disclosure of the presence of God. Participants are invited to be increasingly attentive to the 'hiddeness' in the present moment, to the nuance of what happens in the ambiguous and challenging circumstances of life. This is especially true of Week 5 where the aim is to recognise that one's spirituality affects everything, including all aspects of teaching and learning, to see that God is present and to be discovered in the bits and pieces of everyday life, and to identify practices that can support such a spirituality. It aims to link what people treasure in their lives and from their faith with the core values of the school/parish and to ascertain what it takes to embody them in an ongoing, sustained way. There is an eschatological sense to Week 5 – the kingdom is present, but not quite, not yet. In the same way, the programme is nearing completion and there is a sense of achievement, of closure, of having completed something worthwhile. But there is also a sense that it is only a step, a renewal of something ongoing and eternal. And so one of the hoped-for outcomes of the programme is that participants will want to re-commit in a communal sense to the Catholic faith life of the school and their own spiritual lives. Therefore, Week 5 is sprinkled with opportunities for participants to decide for themselves the route they will follow into the future.

One such route could be the development of a sacramental imagination. Such an imagination has the ability to notice the sacred nature of everything – that everything has the possibility or potential to disclose the divine. It is the ability 'to see', to recognise the presence of God in all things. It is the ability to move beyond a false division between what is sacred and secular – for all is in God. God is the very atmosphere in whom we 'live and move and have our being' (Acts 17:28). The growth of such an imagination will require a particular understanding of grace.

Grace

The human person is reliant on the grace of God (love of God outside of the Trinity) to be open and respond to God's sustained invitation of friendship. In actual fact, the human person is reliant on the grace of God for everything. But it is also possible to refuse grace and act in ways that are opposed to God and to life.

Too often grace has been understood as only available through religious moments in our lives, such as prayer, liturgical events or the visiting of a holy place. These practices were thought to 'fill' the person with grace so that they could withstand and endure the effort it takes to live in a secular world and participate in the public sphere. Gaillardetz puts it well when he says that there has been a strong tendency to see grace as 'something that was "injected" into an otherwise profane world'.[31] However, this is at odds with the theology that has emerged since Vatican II. For Karl Rahner:

> The world is permeated by the grace of God ... The world is constantly and ceaselessly possessed by grace from its innermost roots, from the innermost personal centre of the spiritual subject ... Whether the world gives the impression, so far as our superficial everyday experience is concerned, of being imbued with grace in this way, or whether it constantly seems to give the lie to this state of being permeated by God's grace which it has, this in no sense alters the fact that it is so.[32]

Grace is everywhere, available to all, urging the 'human personality toward expansiveness and self-transcendence'.[33] Since the world is in-grace, God is just as active in our lives while we engage in the public realm (for instance teaching, writing a letter to the paper, meeting parents, speaking on the radio, posting a blog or attending a local meeting), as in the private (for instance when we pray, go to church or attend a religious event). It is not an 'either/or' situation. Rather, formal religious events ought to disclose the all-pervasive presence of God's effective love in our lives and help us through grace to respond in a cooperative manner. This is a central point and fundamental to what happens in *Joining the Dots*. The author Alice Walker in *The Color Purple* gets to the heart of it when one of her characters asks: 'Celie, tell the truth, have you ever found God in church? I never did. I just found a bunch of folks hoping for him to show. Any God I ever felt in church I brought in with me. And I think all the other folks did too. They come to church to share God, not find God.'[34]

The world – a place crammed with heaven

The view articulated by Walker that we 'come to church to share God' presupposes that God is active in our lives both inside and outside the religious sphere. It does not hold with the false separation between what is sacred and what is secular – as if they were two opposing and competing spheres. If the world is in-grace, in-God, then *all* is sacred – there is no sphere that is beyond the embrace of God's love. But coming to experience and recognise this in a conscious and mindful way is often difficult. The American theologian Michael Himes says that since 'God is present everywhere, you and I need to notice, accept, and celebrate that presence somewhere.'[35] This is the function and role of sacraments in our lives. A sacrament (including the seven 'great communal' sacraments) is something that seeks to disclose the presence of grace already in the world and help us to respond to this self-disclosure in appropriate ways. Experiences of people, events, places, encounters can all somehow disclose the sacred depth in life. In other words, everything and anything can be sacramental – reminding us of the constant embrace of God's self-giving love. In her poem 'Aurora Leigh', Elizabeth Barrett Browning makes reference to Moses meeting God at the burning bush; realising he is on holy ground he takes off his shoes. She points to the difference a sacramental imagination can make:

> *Earth's crammed with heaven,*
> *And every common bush afire with God:*
> *But only he who sees, takes off his shoes,*
> *The rest sit round it, and pluck blackberries,*
> *And daub their natural faces unaware*
> *More and more from the first similitude [...]*
>
> *If a man could feel,*
> *Not one day, in the artist's ecstasy,*
> *But every day, feast, fast, or working-day,*

The spiritual significance burn through
The hieroglyphic of material shows,
Henceforth he would paint the globe with wings,
And reverence fish and fowl, the bull, the tree,
And even his very body as a man, –

A sacramental imagination helps us notice the presence of God in the world. Too often we miss the revelatory potential of those places, events and moments that are thought too ordinary, random, unholy, conflictual or abrasive to be disclosive of God or the arena for responding to God.

At this stage, an important caveat needs to be made. While we may speak about the disclosure of God, we need to approach this area with great humility and care. We must always remember that God remains incomprehensible to us, far beyond anything we can imagine. Whatever way we think of God is only a paltry reflection of what and who God is. Great harm has been done by those who feel overly confident that they know God, know what it is that God wants for the world and what God wants them to do about it.

A sacramental imagination not only helps us to see the sacred nature of our lives; it is also concerned with action that is in keeping with the God disclosed in Jesus Christ, whose spirit is at work in the world today. 'Seeing' God demands a response.

Service in the world

'All that I have and possess, you, Lord, have given me. All of it is yours, dispose of it according to your will.'[36] This prayer forms the conclusion of the Spiritual Exercises. Ignatian spirituality understands that the gifts we are given and develop through the opportunities of a holistic education are to be offered in service to the world and ultimately for the Kingdom. Ignatius, like Jesus, invites retreatants to respond with generous desires and generous service. Christian education is gifted with opportunities not only to help others cultivate their gifts and talents in service to the world but to allow educators themselves to put their own gifts and talents to this use. In one sense, educators have already decided what form their service will take. On the other hand, ongoing discernment of the wisdom of that decision as well as dealing with opportunities and decisions that cross their paths is crucial.

The phrase that Ignatius used more than any other in his writings, 'helping souls', encapsulates service as the core of his spirituality – a spiritual as well as physical mandate. This is what the Spiritual Exercises are all about – discerning God's will in one's deepest desires and thus the form of one's service. Of course, if God is in all things, there is no aspect of life or human interest that is inappropriate for Christian service. The early Jesuits went where they saw the greatest needs; 'the world is our home,' said Jeronimo Nadal, one of Ignatius' closest associates. This understanding also affirms the validity of all calls in life – of which education in all its forms and facets is one.

Conclusion

No amount of curriculum innovation, standardised testing, or technological aids are sufficient to make a good school. A school or parish is only as good as its participants – children, young people, parents, auxiliary staff, leaders, and of course, educators. So much depends on the spirits of educators and therefore on what is likely to sustain their spirits. The Catholic Christian tradition is a rich resource and dynamic partner for programmes to nourish spirituality.

Fostering the spiritual lives of educators is crucial; healthy spirituality can be a sustaining force, helping them to thrive rather than simply survive in schools and parishes today. The issue is important both for the personal development of educators themselves and because their spiritual lives dynamically affect the educational life and experience of the whole community, including and perhaps especially the students they teach.

Joining the Dots is about answering educators' own desires for space to reflect on the moments that providentially fill their days. It allows access to age-old methods of discerning these moments: Scripture and tradition and habits of prayer which ask 'how does the word of God speak to me in my experience of life? Where is the Good News in the stuff of every day?' It offers the time and space to remember that even if we are tired of looking for God, God never tires looking for us.

NOTES

1. 'Canal Bank Walk' by Patrick Kavanagh, *Collected Poems*, Antoinette Quinn (ed.) (London: Allen Lane, 2004).

2. See H. Richard Niebuhr, *Christ and Culture* (New York: Harper & Row, 1951).

3. Elaine Graham, Heather Walton and Francis Ward, *Theological Reflection: Methods* (London: SCM Press, 2005), 138.

4. Paul Tillich and James Luther Adams, *Political Expectations* (Macon: Mercer University Press, 1981), 57.

5. Thomas H. Groome, *Sharing Faith: A Comprehensive Approach to Religious Education and Pastoral Ministry: The Way of Shared Praxis*, 1st ed. (San Francisco: HarperSanFrancisco, 1991), 101.

6. Thomas H. Groome, 'Inculturation: How to Proceed in a Pastoral Context', *Concilium* (1994), 121.

7. David Tracy, *Plurality and Ambiguity: Hermeneutics, Religion, Hope* (Chicago: University of Chicago Press, 1994), 19.

8. Hans Georg Gadamer, Joel Weinsheimer and Donald G. Marshall, *Truth and Method*, 2nd rev. ed. (London; New York: Continuum, 2004), 299.

9. 'Text' here is used in its widest sense to include, for instance, a piece of art or music, a memory, a belief or an experience.

10. Michael Cowan and Bernard J. Lee, *Conversation, Risk, and Conversion: The Inner and Public Life of Small Christian Communities* (Maryknoll, New York: Orbis Books, 1997), 85.

11. Ibid.

12. Bernard J. F. Lonergan, *Method in Theology* (New York: Herder and Herder, 1972), 133.

13. Pope Benedict XVI, 'Meeting with the Representatives of British Society, Including the Diplomatic Corps, Politicians, Academics and Business Leaders: Address of His Holiness Benedict XVI' (Westminster Hall: 2010).

14. See Chapter 4.

15. Parker Palmer, 'The Heart of a Teacher: Identity and Integrity in Teaching', *Change* 29, no. 6 (1997), 14.

16. Nicholas Lash, *The Beginning and the End of 'Religion'* (New York: Cambridge University Press, 1996), 174.

17. Sandra Schneiders, 'Religion and Spirituality: Strangers, Rivals or Partners?', *The Santa Clara Lectures* 6, no. 2 (2000), 4.

18. Robert J. Starratt, *Historical Frameworks for Understanding Spirituality: Implications for Contemporary Education* (Boston College, 2007), 21.

19. William A. Barry and Robert G. Doherty, *Contemplatives in Action: The Jesuit Way* (New York: Paulist Press, 2002), 9.

20. Jose Ignacio Tellechea Idígoras, *Ignatius of Loyola: The Pilgrim Saint*, trans. Cornelius Michael Buckley SJ (Chicago: Loyola Press, 1994), 584. Of the very many biographies of Ignatius of Loyola, I use this work as my principal source. Tellechea Idígoras (1928–), likewise a Basque but

non-Jesuit, has the advantage of understanding the culture and context of the early years and formative childhood experiences of Ignatius, and also offers a critical eye to his life, work, shortcomings and inspirations.

21. *Const.*, n. 288. When referring to this bedrock of Ignatian spirituality, I will use the well-known summary phrase 'finding God in all things'.

22. Idígoras, 482.

23. Michael Downey, *Understanding Christian Spirituality* (New York: Paulist Press, 1997), 44–5.

24. Richard R. Gaillardetz, *Transforming Our Days: Spirituality, Community, and Liturgy in a Technological Culture* (New York: Crossroad, 2000), 54–5; italics in original.

25. Michael Himes, 'Contrasting Views of the Church's Mission', in *National Board of Religious Inspectors and Advisors Annual Meeting* (London: 2004).

26. Ibid.

27. Ibid.

28. See John Shea, *Stories of Faith* (Allen, Texas: T. More, 1996).

29. John Shea, *The Hour of the Unexpected*, 1st ed. (Niles, Illinois: Argus Communications, 1977), 68.

30. See Chapter 4.

31. Gaillardetz, 98.

32. As quoted in ibid., 98–9.

33. Roger Haight, *The Experience and Language of Grace* (New York: Paulist Press, 1979), 161.

34. Alice Walker, *The Color Purple* (Boston: G.K. Hall, 1986), 176.

35. Michael J. Himes, *The Mystery of Faith: An Introduction to Catholicism* (Cincinnati, Ohio: St Anthony Messenger Press, 2004), 12.

36. Ignatius Loyola, 'The Spiritual Exercises', in *Spiritual Exercises and Selected Works*, George E. Ganss (ed.) (New York: Paulist Press, 1991), n. 234.

Bibliography

Addresses

Benedict XVI, 'Address to the Participants in the Convention of the Diocese of Rome', Rome, 2011.

Benedict XVI, 'Meeting with the Representative of British Society, Including the Diplomatic Corps, Politicians, Academics and Business Leaders: Address of His Holiness Benedict XVI', Westminster Hall, 2010.

Articles

Coolohan, John, 'Church, State and Education in Contemporary Ireland: Some Perspectives', in *From Present to Future: Catholic Education in Ireland for the New Century*, Eithne Woulfe and James Cassin (eds), Dublin: Veritas, 2006, 88–110.

Goggin, Paula, and Colette McCarthy-Dineen, 'Christianity – Origins and Contemporary Expressions', in *Faith Seeking Understanding*, Micheál de Barra (ed.), Dublin: Veritas, 2005.

Books

Barry, William A., and Robert G. Doherty, *Contemplatives in Action: The Jesuit Way*, New York: Paulist Press, 2002.

Congregation for the Clergy, *General Directory for Catechesis*, Washington DC: United States Catholic Conference, 1997.

Cowan, Michael, and Bernard J. Lee, *Conversation, Risk, and Conversion: The Inner and Public Life of Small Christian Communities*, Maryknoll, New York: Orbis Books, 1997.

Dorr, Donal, *Divine Energy: God Beyond Us, Within Us, Among Us*, Dublin: Gill and Macmillan, 1996.

Downey, Michael, *Understanding Christian Spirituality*, New York: Paulist Press, 1997.

Flannery OP, Austin (ed.), *Vatican Council II: The Basic Sixteen Documents*, Dublin: Dominican Publications, 1996.

Gadamer, Hans Georg, Joel Weinsheimer, and Donald G. Marshall, *Truth and Method*, 2nd rev. ed., London; New York: Continuum, 2004.

Gaillardetz, Richard R., *Transforming Our Days: Spirituality, Community, and Liturgy in a Technological Culture*, New York: Crossroad, 2000.

Graham, Elaine, Heather Walton and Francis Ward, *Theological Reflection: Methods*, London: SCM Press, 2005.

Groome, Thomas H., *Educating for Life: A Spiritual Vision for Every Teacher and Parent*, Allen, Texas: T. More, 1998.

Groome, Thomas H., *Sharing Faith: A Comprehensive Approach to Religious Education and Pastoral Ministry: The Way of Shared Praxis*, 1st ed., San Francisco: Harper SanFrancisco, 1991.

Groome, Thomas H., *Will There Be Faith? Depends on Every Christian*, Dublin: Veritas, 2011.

Haight, Roger, *The Experience and Language of Grace*, New York: Paulist Press, 1979.

Himes, Michael J., *The Mystery of Faith: An Introduction to Catholicism*, Cincinnati, Ohio: St Anthony Messenger Press, 2004.

Idígoras, Jose Ignacio Tellechea, *Ignatius of Loyola: The Pilgrim Saint*, trans. by Cornelius Michael Buckley SJ, Chicago: Loyola Press, 1994.

Irish Catholic Bishops' Conference, *Vision 08: A Vision for Catholic Education in Ireland*, Maynooth: Irish Catholic Bishops' Conference, 2008.

Kavanagh, Patrick, *Collected Poems*, Antoinette Quinn (ed.), London: Allen Lane, 2004.

Lane, Dermot A., *The Experience of God: An Invitation to Do Theology*, rev. ed., New York: Paulist Press, 2005.

Lash, Nicholas, *The Beginning and the End of 'Religion'*, New York: Cambridge University Press, 1996.

Lonergan, Bernard J. F., *Method in Theology*, New York: Herder and Herder, 1972.

Lonsdale, David, *Eyes to See, Ears to Hear: An Introduction to Ignatian Spirituality*, Philip Sheldrake (ed.), Maryknoll, New York: Orbis, 2000.

Loyola, Ignatius, 'The Spiritual Exercises', in *Spiritual Exercises and Selected Works*, George E. Ganss (ed.), New York: Paulist Press, 1991.

Merton, Thomas, and Lynn Szabo, *In the Dark before Dawn: New Selected Poems of Thomas Merton*, New York: New Directions, 2005.

Niebuhr, H. Richard, *Christ and Culture*, New York: Harper & Row, 1951.

Nouwen, Henri J. M., *Reaching Out: The Three Movements of the Spiritual Life*, New York: Doubleday, 1975.

O'Leary, Daniel J., *Begin with the Heart, the Harvest Will Follow: Recovering a Sacramental Vision for Pastoral Ministry and Personal Wholeness*, Dublin: Columba Press, 2008.

Palmer, Parker J., *The Courage to Teach: Exploring the Inner Landscape of a Teacher's Life*, San Francisco: Jossey-Bass, 1998.

Rolheiser, Ronald, *Seeking Spirituality: Guidelines for a Christian Spirituality for the Twenty-First Century*, London: Hodder & Stoughton, 1998.

Shea, John, *Stories of Faith*, Allen, Texas: T. More, 1996.

Shea, John, *The Hour of the Unexpected*, 1st ed., Niles, Illinois: Argus Communications, 1977.

Starratt, Robert J., *Historical Frameworks for Understanding Spirituality: Implications for Contemporary Education*, Boston College, 2007.

Tillich, Paul, and James Luther Adams, *Political Expectations*, Macon: Mercer University Press, 1981.

Tracy, David, *Plurality and Ambiguity: Hermeneutics, Religion, Hope*, Chicago: University of Chicago Press, 1994.

Walker, Alice, *The Color Purple*, Boston: G.K. Hall, 1986.

Journals

Groome, Thomas H., 'Inculturation: How to Proceed in a Pastoral Context', in *Concilium* (1994), 120–33.

Himes, Michael, 'Contrasting Views of the Church's Mission', in *National Board of Religious Inspectors and Advisors Annual Meeting Papers*, London, 2004.

Palmer, Parker, 'The Heart of a Teacher: Identity and Integrity in Teaching', in *Change* 29, no. 6 (1997), 14–21.

Schneiders, Sandra, 'Religion and Spirituality: Strangers, Rivals or Partners?', in *The Santa Clara Lectures* 6, no. 2 (2000), 1–26.

Websites

Ashton-Warner, Sylvia, http://www.quotes.net/authors/Sylvia+Ashton-Warner%2c+Spinster

Auden, W. H., http://www.quotes.net/authors/Wystan+Hugh+Auden

Gandhi, Mahatma, http://quotationsbook.com/quote/16086/

Cassels, Louis, 'A Christmas Parable', The Derry Diocese Catechetical Centre, http:/www.catecheticalcentre.org/index.php?pg=12&thought_id=18

Ignatian Spirituality, http://www.ignatianspirituality.com

Lawler, Philip F., 'Pew Survey Shows America's Vast Catholic Exodus', http://www.catholicculture.org/news/features/index.cfm/recnum=56894

Rolheiser Ronald, http://www.ronrolheiser.com

Sarkozy, Nicolas, 'A Letter to Educators: President Sarkozy Writes to French Teachers and Parents', http://www.ambafrance-uk.org/President-Sarkozy-writes-to-French.html

Shakespeare, William, *Hamlet*, Act I, Scene III, http://www.enotes.com/shakespeare-quotes/thine-own-self-true

Tolkien, J. R., *The Hobbit*, Wisdom Quotes http://www.wisdomquotes.com/quote/j-r-r-tolkien.html

Tzu Lao, http://www.quotes.net/quote/3741

The Examen of Consciousness: www.sluh.org/campus/pastoralministry/theexamenofconsciousness

'The Universality of the Golden Rule in World Religions', http://www.teachingvalues.com/goldenrule.html

Vassilikou Bicouvaris, Mary, http://www.inspirationalquotes4u.com/inspirationalquotesteacher/index.html

Williams, Margery, *The Velveteen Rabbit*, Doubleday, http://digital.library.upenn.edu/women/williams/rabbit/rabbit.html